Key Concepts
in
American History

Isolationism

Set Contents

Key Concepts in American History

Abolitionism

Colonialism

Expansionism

Federalism

Industrialism

Internationalism

Isolationism

Nationalism

Progressivism

Terrorism

Key Concepts in American History

Isolationism

Tom Streissguth
Lora Friedenthal

Jennifer L. Weber, Ph.D.
General Editor
University of Kansas

CHELSEA HOUSE
PUBLISHERS
An imprint of Infobase Publishing

Key Concepts in American History: Isolationism

DEVELOPED, DESIGNED, AND PRODUCED BY DWJ BOOKS LLC

Chelsea House
An imprint of Infobase Publishing
132 West 31st Street
New York NY 10001

Library of Congress Cataloging-in-Publication Data

Streissguth, Thomas, 1958–
    Isolationism / Tom Streissguth, Lora Friedenthal ; Jennifer L. Weber, general editor.
        p. cm. – (Key concepts in American history)
    Includes bibliographical references and index.
    ISBN 978-1-60413-224-3 (hardcover)
1. United States—Foreign relations—20th century—Encyclopedias, Juvenile. 2. Isolationism—United States—History—20th century—Encyclopedias, Juvenile. I. Friedenthal, Lora.
II. Weber, Jennifer L., 1962– III. Title. IV. Series.
    E744.S943 2009
    327.10973–dc22
                        2009025285

Chelsea House books are available at special discounts when purchased in bulk quantities for businesses, associations, institutions, or sales promotions. Please call our Special Sales Department in New York at (212) 967-8800 or (800) 322-8755.

You can find Chelsea House on the World Wide Web at http://www.chelseahouse.com

Cover printed by Bang Printing, Brainerd, MN
Book printed and bound by Bang Printing, Brainerd, MN
Date printed: May 2010
Printed in the United States of America

10 9 8 7 6 5 4 3 2 1

This book is printed on acid-free paper.

Acknowledgments
pp. 1, 49, 56, 64, 74, 96: The Granger Collection, New York; p. 17: Library of Congress, Prints and Photographs Division; p. 19: Private Collection/The Stapleton Collection/The Bridgeman Art Library; p. 36: Private Collection/Peter Newark Historical Pictures/The Bridgeman Art Library; p. 79: Private Collection/The Bridgeman Art Library.

Contents

List of Illustrations vi

Reader's Guide to
Isolationism vii

Milestones in Isolationism
(1920–Present) viii

Preface x

What Is Isolationism? 1

Isolationism from A to Z

America First Committee
(AFC) 11

Appeasement, Policy of 13

Axis Powers 14

Borah, William E. (1865–1940) 16

Central Powers 18

Coolidge, Calvin (1872–1933) 20

Dawes Plan 22

Democratic Party 23

History Makers: Franklin D.
Roosevelt (1882–1945) 24

Emergency Quota Act (1921) 25

Fourteen Points 26

History Speaks: Wilson's
Plan for International
Cooperation 28

France 30

Great Britain 32

Harding, Warren G.
(1865–1923) 34

Hitler, Adolf (1889–1945) 35

Japan 38

Kellogg-Briand Pact (1928) 40

Ku Klux Klan 42

League of Nations 43

Then & Now: Authority of
the League vs. the UN 45

Lend-Lease Act (1941) 46

Lindbergh, Charles A.
(1902–1974) 48

Lodge, Henry Cabot
(1850–1924) 51

Monroe Doctrine 53

History Speaks: Protecting
the Hemisphere 54

Mussolini, Benito (1883–1945) 55

National Origins Act (1924) 58

Nye, Gerald P. (1892–1971) 60

Palmer Raids 61

Pearl Harbor 63

Then & Now: Pearl Harbor
and 9/11 65

Red Scare 69

History Speaks: Justifying
the Panic 70

Republican Party 71

Reservationists 73

Russian Revolution and
Civil War 74

Smoot-Hawley Tariff 76

Thomas, Norman
(1884–1968) 77

Treaty of Versailles (1919) 78

History Speaks:
Establishing the League 82

War Reparations 84

Washington's Farewell
Address 85

Wilson, Woodrow
(1856–1924) 86

World War I (1914–1918) 90

World War II (1939–1945) 94

Young Plan 97

Viewpoints About Isolationism

Asking Congress for War,
Woodrow Wilson, 1917 99

From the Shantung Clause,
1919 101

From the Peace for Our
Time Speech, Prime Minister
Neville Chamberlain, 1938 102

Speaking Against Involvement,
Charles A. Lindbergh,
September 11, 1941 103

From the Lend-Lease Act,
1941 105

Glossary of Key Terms 109
Selected Bibliography 113
Index 116

List of Illustrations

Photos

Signing of the U.S.
Constitution 1

William E. Borah 17

Kaiser Wilhelm II 19

Hitler speaks at Nazi Party
rally 36

Charles Lindbergh 49

Benito Mussolini and Adolf
Hitler, 1937 56

Attack on Pearl Harbor 64
The Winter Palace in Russia 74
The Treaty of Versailles 79
D-day invasion of Normandy 96

Maps

World War I 93
World War II 95

Reader's Guide
to Isolationism

The list that follows is provided as an aid to readers in locating articles on the big topics or themes in isolationism, the foreign policy that guided the United States for much of its history. The Reader's Guide arranges all of the A to Z entries in *Key Concepts in American History: Isolationism* according to these **6 key concepts** of the social studies curriculum: **Economics and Trade**; **Government and Law**; **Nations**; **People and Society**; **Policies and Programs**; and **Wars and Battles**. Some articles appear in more than one category to help link topics.

Economics and Trade
America First Committee
Dawes Plan
Smoot-Hawley Tariff
War Reparations
Young Plan

Government and Law
Democratic Party
Emergency Quota Act (1921)
Fourteen Points
Kellogg-Briand Pact (1928)
League of Nations
Lend-Lease Act (1941)
Monroe Doctrine
National Origins Act (1924)
Palmer Raids
Red Scare
Republican Party
Reservationists
Russian Revolution and
  Civil War
Treaty of Versailles (1919)
War Reparations

Nations
Axis Powers
Central Powers

France
Great Britain
Japan
League of Nations
Monroe Doctrine
Russian Revolution and
  Civil War
Treaty of Versailles (1919)

People and Society
America First Committee
Borah, William E. (1865–1940)
Coolidge, Calvin (1872–1933)
Fourteen Points
Harding, Warren G.
  (1865–1923)
Hitler, Adolf (1889–1945)
Ku Klux Klan
League of Nations
Lindbergh, Charles A.
  (1902–1974)
Lodge, Henry Cabot
  (1850–1924)
Mussolini, Benito (1883–1945)
Nye, Gerald P. (1892–1971)
Palmer Raids
Red Scare
Reservationists

Russian Revolution and
  Civil War
Thomas, Norman
  (1884–1968)
Wilson, Woodrow
  (1856–1924)

Policies and Programs
Appeasement, Policy of
Dawes Plan
League of Nations
Monroe Doctrine
Palmer Raids
Reservationists
Washington's Farewell
  Address
Young Plan

Wars and Battles
Axis Powers
Central Powers
Hitler, Adolf (1889–1945)
Pearl Harbor
Russian Revolution and
  Civil War
War Reparations
World War I (1914–1918)
World War II (1939–1945)

Milestones in

As a young nation, the United States limited its involvement in world affairs—focusing mostly on trade issues. Only when the nation's vital interests were threatened did the United States react with military force.

After World War I (1914–1918), most Americans wanted to keep the country apart, or isolated, from the world's problems to prevent the United States from being dragged into another horrific war. This policy of isolationism lasted until 1941, when the Japanese Empire attacked the U.S. military base in Pearl Harbor, Hawaii. The United States had no choice but to react and end its **isolationist** foreign policy.

1796 George Washington (1789–1797) issues his farewell address, warning the young United States to avoid "entangling alliances."

1812 War of 1812 (1812–1814) with Great Britain begins.

1823 President James Monroe (1817–1825) issues the Monroe Doctrine, warning European powers to stay out of the Western Hemisphere.

1912 Woodrow Wilson (1913–1921) is elected the 28th president of the United States.

1914 World War I (1914–1918) breaks out in Europe.

1916 Wilson is reelected on the theme "He Kept Us Out of War."

1917 The United States enters World War I on the side of the Allies.

1918 Germany signs an armistice on November 11, ending World War I.

1920 Warren G. Harding (1921–1923) is elected the 29th president of the United States, promising a "return to normalcy."

1921 U.S. Senate rejects the Treaty of Versailles and refuses to join the League of Nations; Red Scare, a fear of a Communist takeover of the U.S. government, grips the nation.

1922 Fascist dictator Benito Mussolini (1922–1943) assumes power in Italy.

1923 President Harding dies suddenly; Calvin Coolidge (1923–1929) assumes office and continues Harding's isolationist policies.

1928 Kellogg-Briand Pact outlaws war as a tool of foreign policy; Herbert Hoover (1929–1933) is elected the 31st president of the United States.

1929 Great Depression causes economic hardship worldwide.

1930 Congress passes Smoot-Hawley Act, which raises tariffs on more than 20,000 imported goods; international trade plunges.

1931 Japan invades the Chinese province of Manchuria.

Isolationism (1920–Present)

1932 Franklin D. Roosevelt (1933–1945) is elected the 32nd president of the United States; Roosevelt implements New Deal to try to end the Great Depression.

1933 Adolf Hitler (1933–1945) is elected chancellor of Germany; Hitler and his Nazi Party seize control of entire German government.

1935 U.S. Congress passes the first of several Neutrality Acts designed to keep the nation out of foreign wars.

1938 Germany annexes the Sudetenland, a part of Czechoslovakia with a large German ethnic population; Germany annexes Austria.

1939 Germany invades Poland on September 1; France and Great Britain declare war on Germany on September 3; the United States declares its neutrality.

1941 U.S. Congress passes the Lend-Lease Act, providing aid to the Allies; Japan attacks Pearl Harbor, Hawaii, bringing the United States into World War II.

1945 World War II ends; United Nations (UN) is organized; United States emerges from the war as a superpower and permanently ends the nation's isolationist foreign policy.

2001 Al Qaeda terrorists hijack four American jetliners and crash them into the World Trade Center in New York City; the Pentagon in Washington, D.C.; and a field in Pennsylvania— more than 3,000 civilians are killed; "war on terror" begins when the United States invades Afghanistan.

2003 The United States and its allies invade Iraq and sustain a costly, increasingly unpopular, and controversial war.

2008 Barack Obama (2009–) is elected the 44th president of the United States. Obama promises to begin withdrawing American troops from Iraq in 2010; sends additional forces into Afghanistan in 2009.

2009 Barack Obama announces plans to withdraw most American troops from Iraq; the president details his plan to build up American forces in Afghanistan but turn over more responsibility to Afghan forces.

Preface

The United States was founded on ideas. Those who wrote the U.S. Constitution were influenced by ideas that began in Europe: reason over religion, human rights over the rights of kings, and self-governance over tyranny. Ideas, and the arguments over them, have continued to shape the nation. Of all the ideas that influenced the nation's founding and its growth, 10 are perhaps the most important and are singled out here in an original series—KEY CONCEPTS IN AMERICAN HISTORY. The volumes bring these concepts to life, *Abolitionism, Colonialism, Expansionism, Federalism, Industrialism, Internationalism, Isolationism, Nationalism, Progressivism*, and *Terrorism*.

These books examine the big ideas, major events, and influential individuals that have helped define American history. Each book features three sections. The first is an overview of the concept, its historical context, the debates over the concept, and how it changed the history and growth of the United States. The second is an encyclopedic, A-to-Z treatment of the people, events, issues, and organizations that help to define the "-ism" under review. Here, readers will find detailed facts and vivid histories, along with referrals to other books for more details about the topic.

Interspersed throughout the entries are many high-interest features: "History Speaks" provides excerpts of documents, speeches, and letters from some of the most influential figures in American history. "History Makers" provides brief biographies of key people who dramatically influenced the country. "Then and Now" helps readers connect issues of the nation's past with present-day concerns.

In the third part of each volume, "Viewpoints," readers will find longer primary documents illustrating ideas that reflect a certain point of view of the time. Also included are important government documents and key Supreme Court decisions.

The KEY CONCEPTS series also features "Milestones in. . . ," time lines that will enable readers to quickly sort out how one event led to another, a glossary, and a bibliography for further reading.

People make decisions that determine history, and Americans have generated and refined the ideas that have determined U.S. history. With an understanding of the most important concepts that have shaped our past, readers can gain a better idea of what has shaped our present.

Jennifer L. Weber, Ph.D.
Assistant Professor of History, University of Kansas
General Editor

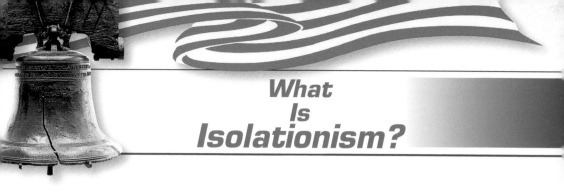

What Is Isolationism?

The roots of isolationism in the United States can be traced back to the American Revolution (1775–1783). Those who favored independence from Great Britain believed they should set themselves apart, or remain isolated, from Europe and its oppressive monarchies, nations ruled by all-powerful kings or queens.

The victory against the British army and the **ratification** of the U.S. Constitution established the United States as a republic—a country in which people rule through elected representatives and an elected president. Such a country, according to its early leaders, could be not only independent but also self-sufficient. The nation's early leaders intended that the country stay clear of Europe's age-old conflicts. By practicing a policy of isolationism, they believed the new republic would not take part in the tangled agreements that so often ensnared European nations in war.

EARLY ACTIONS

The first president, George Washington (1789–1797), explained the country's **isolationist** policy clearly in his 1796 farewell address, given just before he left office. In his speech, he warned the young nation to stay out of entangling alliances.

Representatives of 12 of the 13 states signed the U.S. Constitution in Philadelphia, Pennsylvania, in 1787. Later, from 1789–1797, George Washington (standing, right) served as the country's first president. In his Farewell Address, he advised those who followed him to keep the nation free of foreign entanglements.

Other early presidents, including John Adams (1797–1801) and Thomas Jefferson (1801–1809), found that European conflicts sometimes interfered with other U.S. policies. For example, during Great Britain's war with the French emperor Napoleon Bonaparte in the early 1800s, American sailors were often **impressed**, or kidnapped, into the British navy. This was one grievance among many that led to the War of 1812 (1812–1814) with the British. The Barbary pirates of North Africa raided American ships, kidnapping and holding American citizens for **ransom**. President Jefferson ordered the U.S. Navy to take action against these pirates in the Mediterranean Sea. In fact, Jefferson was the first president to forcefully project American military power into a distant locale. Yet, Jefferson did not seek this military action. He responded only when the nation's economic interests were challenged.

A RISING POWER

In 1823, with the issuance of the Monroe Doctrine, the United States declared that European nations had no right to interfere in the nations of the Western Hemisphere. Many early American leaders believed that the United States would one day expand across North America. By the 1840s, in the words of newspaper editor John O'Sullivan, it was the nation's **"manifest destiny"** to conquer the continent. The thousands of settlers moving west along the Ohio and Missouri rivers heartily agreed. The United States had become increasingly powerful, seeking new land and resources. With the expansion of the country, however, isolationism became more difficult.

MOVING WEST

In western North America, the United States contended with foreign nations for land, resources, and political control. It also fought the many Native American peoples who sought to defend their ways of life. British Canada and Russia had claims on Alaska and the Pacific Northwest. Mexican settlers were living in the southwest part of the country and Texas. The victory in the Mexican-American War (1846–1848) allowed the United States to add vast new reaches of western North America to its territory. In 1898, the United States defeated Spain in the Spanish-American War (1898). As a result, Cuba gained independence—with a great deal of American political influence—and the United States colonized the Philippines off the eastern coast of Asia.

World War I Although the nation was industrializing, expanding its territory, and asserting its military power, politicians and influential editors often cried out "America First!" The notion won further support when, in the summer of 1914, a tangled web of military alliances dragged the nations of Europe into World War I (1914–1918). At first, the United States remained **neutral**, following the recommendation of President Woodrow Wilson (1913–1921), who saw no vital national interest at stake. Neutrality, however, did not prevent attacks by German submarines on American shipping, nor did it suit the American self-image as an emerging and important nation, an essential actor on the stage of world events.

War! In spring 1915, a German submarine attacked the *Lusitania,* a British passenger liner, off the coast of Ireland. More than 1,000 civilians were killed. The attack and resulting deaths convinced many that the United States could not remain neutral and should retaliate. In April 1917, Wilson asked Congress to declare war against Germany. Thus, the United States joined in the fight on the side of the Allies, which included Great Britain, France, and Russia.

ISOLATIONISM BETWEEN THE WARS

After the end of World War I, the U.S. Senate rejected the Treaty of Versailles, which set the terms of the peace and created the League of Nations, which President Wilson strongly supported. Opponents of the treaty, led by senators William Borah and Henry Cabot Lodge, helped keep the United States out of the league. Politicians opposed to the league did not want to see the United States become the "world's policeman." The terrible toll of World War I, with the ravaged countryside of northern

France and the millions of military and civilian deaths in western and eastern Europe, hardened public opinion against any future significant involvement in world affairs. Author Paul Johnson places the blame squarely on the shoulders of Woodrow Wilson:

> The [isolationism of the] interwar period, however, is [not] the norm in America's relationship with the world . . . The blame must rest primarily with Wilson's arrogant obstinacy, and then with his sick state of mind, which [made him insist] that the treaty he had negotiated at Versailles . . . be ratified unamended.

Increasing Isolationist Feelings The failure of the Treaty of Versailles in the U.S. Senate turned the country away from Europe. Isolationist sentiment strengthened groups such as the Ku Klux Klan. The Klan had begun in the South, just after the Civil War (1861–1865), to oppose **Reconstruction** and the **emancipation** of the slaves. Klan members saw themselves as patriots. The Klan's anti-**immigrant** sentiment gave the organization nationwide appeal. At the time, many Americans saw foreigners as threatening their ideals. The slogan "America First!" ran strong, particularly in the Midwest, where a common sentiment was that the old nations of Europe were hopelessly corrupt and that World War I had been fought on behalf of wealthy industrialists, bankers, and weapons makers on both sides of the Atlantic.

Limited Contact Although they wanted to avoid entanglements in world affairs, isolationists did not want to see the United States cut itself off entirely from the rest of the world. Political leaders knew that foreign trade was essential to the American economy. Within limits, which grew stricter during the 1920s, Congress also allowed **immigration** to the United States. Twice during the 1920s, American diplomats helped create new plans that changed the terms of the peace established by the Treaty of Versailles by rescheduling the war **reparations** Germany had to pay for having started World War I.

In fact, the United States played a role as a mediator in many international diplomatic conferences.

Still, the United States, according to its presidents, legislators, and the press of the 1920s, was to remain wary of any treaties and alliances, even with traditional allies. "The business of America is business," said President Calvin Coolidge (1923–1929) in a 1925 speech. Many agreed with Coolidge, and the prosperity of the 1920s reinforced the idea that the country could truly be self-sufficient. Americans believed that the United States best served the cause of peace by minding its own business and setting an example of **democracy** and free-market **capitalism** for the rest of the world.

ANSWERING GERMANY AND JAPAN

During the 1930s, the **Great Depression** threw the world economy into decline. This event was touched off by the crash of the U.S. stock market in October 1929. Millions of workers lost their jobs. In an effort to protect manufacturing businesses, the U.S. Senate passed high **tariffs**, or taxes on imported goods. This caused a drop in foreign trade and resulted in economic hardship all over the world.

American **democracy** was not followed in Europe, where German resentment at the harsh terms of the Versailles Treaty led to the rise of the Nazi dictator Adolf Hitler (r. 1933–1945). After winning a democratic election in 1933, Hitler was determined to expand German territory and seek revenge for the humiliating defeat of World War I. By rearming itself under Hitler's direction, Germany openly defied the terms of the Versailles Treaty. When Hitler joined with the Italian dictator Benito Mussolini (r. 1922–1943) and with Japan, the stage was set for another global conflict, with or without the participation of the United States.

Neutrality Acts As the political conflicts among the nations of Europe intensified, the U.S. Congress took action to prevent a repeat of the World War I experience. "Nonintervention" was a policy supported by President Franklin D. Roosevelt's (1933–1945) Republican opponents, as well as many Democrats and the public at large. The nation did not want to repeat the World War I experience, in which U.S. troops had fought and died to help Europe resolve another one of its endless political conflicts. Over Roosevelt's opposition, Congress passed a series of Neutrality Acts designed to keep the nation from becoming involved in the affairs of other nations. Knowing where public opinion lay, Roosevelt signed the new laws.

The Neutrality Act of 1935 banned the trade in arms and ammunition with any country participating in a war. Italy was the first country affected, after its dictator, Benito Mussolini, ordered the invasion of the African nation of Ethiopia. In 1936, Congress renewed the ban and also prohibited loans to warring countries.

In 1937, the Neutrality Acts were changed to cover civil wars as well. With this provision, the United States could not trade with either side in the Spanish Civil War (1936–1939), in which U.S. citizens dedicated to the anti-Fascist side took part. By the new law, citizens of the United States could not travel on the ships of warring nations, and no ships were permitted to bring products or passengers to these nations.

Preparing for War In keeping with the U.S. policy of isolationism, the Neutrality Acts were designed to keep the United States out of foreign conflicts. The effort failed, however. President Roosevelt believed that the United States had to take sides when one nation was clearly wronged by another. Japan's invasion of China, for example, prompted Roosevelt to work around the Neutrality Acts by allowing American companies to ship arms to China from the United States aboard British ships.

The Neutrality Acts also failed to deter power-obsessed Adolf Hitler and prevent war in Europe. Hitler forced the unification of Austria and Germany in early 1938. Later in the year, he ordered troops into the Sudetenland, in western Czechoslovakia. The leaders of Britain and France attempted to head off war by agreeing to this occupation of the Sudetenland. Their efforts to appease Hitler proved useless. The German army occupied the rest of Czechoslovakia in March 1939.

On September 1, 1939, Germany invaded Poland, and three days later, Great Britain and France declared war on Germany. In 1941, the Lend-Lease Act allowed the United States to send arms, ammunition, and ships to the British. The stance of neutrality ended, and with the attack on Pearl Harbor by the Japanese on December 7, 1941, the United States entered the war.

THE COLD WAR

America's policy of isolationism ended with the attack on Pearl Harbor. In 1945, World War II (1939–1945) concluded with the formal surrender of Japan. The Soviet Union, Britain, France, and the United States occupied Germany and divided the German capital of Berlin as well as Germany itself. The United States became one of the world's two superpowers, and the nation saw its interests clashing with those of the **Communist** Soviet government. To keep European nations with democratically elected leaders free from economic chaos, the U.S. government helped rebuild cities and industries with loans and grants of money, an operation known as the Marshall Plan. In central and eastern Europe, Soviet-allied governments took power and isolated themselves, as much as possible, from the nations of western Europe.

The doctrine of isolationism fell by the wayside. The victory in World War II had given the United States a sense of mastery over world events. The country saw itself as defending all democratic governments against the Soviet threat of establishing worldwide communism. In the early 1950s, American troops fought in Korea against Soviet-backed forces of North Korea and Communist China. In the 1960s and 1970s, the United States fought to prevent a Communist government from taking power in South Vietnam. Nonetheless, the Communist North Vietnamese toppled South Vietnam, and the United States endured a humiliating withdrawal.

Questioning America's Role After the fall of South Vietnam in 1975, a "Vietnam syndrome," in which the public strongly opposed any further military action in foreign countries, whether or not those countries were under threat of a Communist occupation, prevailed for a generation. When the Soviet Union invaded Afghanistan in December 1979, the United States took part by sending arms to the **insurgents** to fight Soviet troops, tanks, and helicopters. This effort finally succeeded in 1989, when the Soviet army withdrew from Afghanistan. The Soviet defeat in Afghanistan was the first of several military and economic crises that eventually contributed to the collapse of the Soviet Union in December 1991.

End of the Cold War The end of the Cold War in 1991 gave many in the United States a false confidence that an era of international peace had arrived. The role of "world policeman" was one the United States took on with reluctance. Yet neither President George H.W. Bush (1989–1993) nor President Bill Clinton (1993–2001) could ignore trouble in foreign countries. In the Persian Gulf War (1991), the United States and a **coalition** of allies ended the occupation of Kuwait by Iraq, which had invaded the small, oil-rich nation the previous year. The United States sent troops to Somalia, in East Africa, to impose peace during a chaotic civil war and also carried out bombing campaigns in Yugoslavia, located on the Balkan Peninsula, when that country fought a bitter ethnic war. In Somalia and the Balkans, the isolationist debate simmered again within the United States. Many questioned the wisdom of fighting in distant lands, in places where the country had no vital interests at stake.

THE WAR ON TERRORISM
On September 11, 2001, members of an international terrorist group known as al Qaeda struck the United States. The terrorists **hijacked** two passenger jets and flew them deliberately into the Twin Towers of the World Trade Center in New York City; a third plane crashed into the Pentagon just outside of Washington, D.C.; and a fourth hijacked

plane, most likely headed for the White House or the Capitol, crashed in a field in Pennsylvania. Nearly 3,000 people, most of them civilians, died that day as a result of these horrible attacks.

Al Qaeda operated from bases in Afghanistan, where American-armed insurgents had defeated the Soviet occupation. From a series of small, isolated camps in the Afghan countryside, al Qaeda leaders had trained and prepared their followers to commit acts of terrorism against the United States and other Western nations. Their ultimate goal was a war between Muslim and non-Muslim forces in the Middle East, which would ultimately result in the establishment of a new state ruled in accordance with strict Islamic principles.

Terrorism Ends Isolationism Forever The 9/11 attacks ended any illusion that the United States, with its unmatched economic strength and influence, could stay out of foreign conflicts or prevent them from affecting its citizens at home. The collapse of the Soviet Union had changed the terms of global conflicts. In the war on terrorism, there were no battlefronts or campaigns to seize territory, national capitals, and resources.

Historical Roots The roots of this seemingly new global war actually lay centuries in the past, with the expansion of Islam from its homeland in Arabia to North Africa and southern Europe—an event that occurred in the eighth century. The conflict between Islam and Christianity flared during the Christian Crusades of the Middle Ages. Throughout the centuries, Christians fought to regain control of the Holy Land—the land where Jesus is said to have lived and died—from the Arab Muslims who had conquered the area. During the bloody battles of the Crusades, thousands of soldiers and civilians died on both sides.

Later, in the early twentieth century, the Middle East was colonized by the British and the French. The traditional birthplace and spiritual home of Islam, Saudi Arabia, had become a close American ally, and its leaders allowed American troops to be stationed on its soil. The presence of American troops in Saudi Arabia, combined with the strict Islamist view that Western culture and civilization were corrupt and sinful, helped to fuel the terrorists' animosity toward the nations of the West.

A PERMANENT END TO ISOLATIONISM

In the nineteenth century, it had been possible to believe in isolating the country from trouble abroad. The presence of two vast oceans and friendly countries to the north and south protected the United States from invasion. As the United States grew to superpower status after World War II, however, its interests expanded around the world, as did the allies and resources that it had to protect. Although the ideal of a self-sufficient country remains, very few political leaders believe in isolationism.

Throughout the twentieth century and into the twenty-first, the world has become increasingly interdependent. In addition, communication time is now almost instantaneous. Cable television and the Internet immediately broadcast events in Asia, Europe, Africa, and the Americas. The closely linked economies of the world's most powerful nations give those countries both common interests and common problems. Today, the United States cannot be protected by oceans, nor can its leaders refuse to ratify international treaties or keep its military out of foreign conflicts. Instead, foreign conflicts and entanglements will continue to come ashore, demanding a rapid response.

FURTHER READING

Boyer, Paul S., Clifford Clark, Sandra Hawley, Joseph F. Kett, and Andrew Rieser. *The Enduring Vision: A History of the American People. Vol. 2: From 1865.* Wadsworth Publishing, 2009.

Herring, George C. *From Colony to Superpower: U.S. Foreign Relations Since 1776.* New York: Oxford University Press, 2008.

Loewen, James W. *Lies My Teacher Told Me: Everything Your American History Textbook Got Wrong.* New York: Simon & Schuster, 2007.

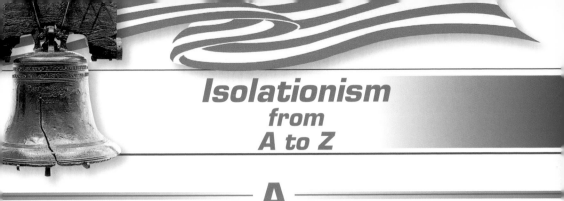

Isolationism
from
A to Z

America First Committee (AFC)

Group opposed to U.S. involvement in World War II (1939–1945), and which insisted on a policy of isolationism as the war spread through western Europe. Two Yale scholars, R. Douglas Stuart and Kingman Brewster, founded the America First Committee in September 1940. The group drew on the widespread **isolationist** sentiment that had been running strong in the United States since the end of World War I (1914–1918).

Soon after its founding, the America First Committee and the cause of **nonintervention** gained widespread support, especially among opponents of President Franklin D. Roosevelt (1933–1945). Local chapters of the AFC, many of them on college campuses, were founded around the country. The group raised money from wealthy donors as well as dues-paying members. The AFC had many supporters in the Chicago region, where its national headquarters was located and where it had the backing of Robert McCormick, the wealthy and influential publisher of the *Chicago Tribune*. The Chicago store tycoon Robert Wood, chairman of the board of Sears Roebuck, became head of the national organization.

GROWTH OF THE AFC

Eventually, the AFC grew to include 850,000 members in 450 chapters. The group sponsored articles and appearances by legislators, business leaders, and celebrities, including author Sinclair Lewis, auto manufacturer Henry Ford, World War I flying ace Eddie Rickenbacker, and cartoonist Walt Disney. Aviator Charles Lindbergh was by far the group's most prominent member. In 1927, Lindbergh had become the first pilot to fly solo across the Atlantic Ocean. This feat made him one of the most popular and recognizable figures in the nation.

The AFC also gained the support of several senators, including Gerald Nye of North Dakota, William Borah of Idaho, Burton Wheeler of Montana, and Robert "Fighting Bob" La Follette of Wisconsin. These senators shared a strong dislike toward Eastern business interests and a suspicion that big business was manipulating public opinion and promoting intervention for its own benefit. Nye in particular was outspoken and adamant on the issue, stating memorably that "To take care of our own [is] the number one American obligation."

Instead of military intervention, the AFC supported a buildup of homeland defenses, making the

United States impregnable to foreign attack. After World War II broke out in Europe, the group opposed a quickening military buildup within the United States. The AFC also opposed the Lend-Lease program, which was passed by Congress in the spring of 1941 to help the **Allies** with much-needed ships and war material. The North Atlantic Ocean, where Lend-Lease ships usually sailed, was the scene of frequent attacks by German submarines. AFC leaders saw Lend-Lease as an attempt to provoke a confrontation and pull the United States into direct conflict with Germany.

MOVES TOWARD WAR
In the years leading up to the war, public opinion in the United States stood against the Nazi dictatorship and German **annexations** of Austria and the Sudetenland region of Czechoslovakia. However, military intervention was opposed by a strong majority of the public, an opinion that changed little as Germany overran France and much of the rest of western Europe in spring 1940. As Britain was left to defend itself without European allies, members of the AFC spoke out stridently against any form of aid.

Lindbergh made a series of speeches broadcast nationally via radio. He criticized the Roosevelt administration's preparations for war and insisted that a group of government leaders, British diplomats, **internationalist** bankers, industrialists, and Jewish leaders were urging the country toward intervention. For many people, Lindbergh's heroic character lent a patriotic stamp to membership in the AFC.

However, Lindbergh's increasingly harsh speeches, with their outright support for Nazi Germany and their poorly disguised **anti-Semitism**, or hatred of the Jews, troubled many. Those favoring involvement questioned the motives of AFC leaders and did not hesitate to point out the anti-American **communist** and **socialist** elements that made up a large base of AFC support. In May 1940, the interventionists answered the AFC with the Committee to Defend America by Aiding the Allies.

U.S. ENTRY INTO THE WAR
When the Japanese attacked U.S. military bases on Pearl Harbor, Hawaii, on December 7, 1941, Roosevelt immediately asked Congress to declare war. Its cause discredited in the face of Japanese aggression, the America First Committee promptly disbanded. Public opinion swung toward support of the war effort, and many isolationists in Congress found themselves outvoted on new legislation. The America First Committee, in the public mind, was soon associated with appeasement of Germany and cowardice in the face of a moral imperative: the defense of **democracy** in Europe and the defeat of a murderous dictatorship.

See also: Appeasement, Policy of; Borah, William E.; Lend-Lease Act; Lindbergh, Charles A.; Nye, Gerald E.; Thomas, Norman; World War II.

FURTHER READING
Berg, A. Scott. *Lindbergh.* New York: Putnam, 1998.

Kauffman, Bill. *America First! Its History, Culture, and Politics.* Amherst, N.Y.: Prometheus Books, 1995.

Lindbergh, Charles A. *The Spirit of St. Louis.* New York: Scribner, 2003.

Anarchists

See Palmer Raids; Red Scare.

Anti-Comintern Pact

See Axis Powers.

Appeasement, Policy of

Approach to settling conflicts by meeting the demands of an opponent. Appeasement was popular among governments after World War I (1914–1918), a long and destructive conflict that moved the United States, and its allies in Europe, to favor negotiation over confrontation. At the outbreak of World War II (1939–1945), however, **isolationists** lost public support by their association with appeasement and its failure to prevent another global conflict.

The Treaty of Versailles that ended World War I also established the League of Nations, an organization meant to foster cooperation among the nations. **Disarmament**, in the common view, would make war less likely, while hostile military action would be met with **blockades** and other measures that would cause great expense to aggressors. Without the credible threat of military force, however, this approach failed to deter the Axis powers, including Japan, Germany, and Italy. As a result, appeasement was discredited as a foreign policy for the rest of the twentieth century.

EARLY HISTORY

Many historians trace the modern history of the appeasement policy to 1931, when Japan, a member of the League of Nations, invaded Manchuria, a northern province of China. The league demanded that Japan withdraw its forces, a request that the Japanese government ignored. When the league officially condemned Japan for its invasion, the Japanese government withdrew from the organization and continued its occupation unopposed.

In 1936, under the leadership of Adolf Hitler (1933–1945), Nazi Germany ordered military units into the Rhineland, a region of Germany that had been declared off-limits to the German army by the Treaty of Versailles. Protests and threats by France and Great Britain had no effect, and the league was unable to agree on economic **sanctions** against Germany for violating the treaty. Without a credible military threat to check his aggression, Hitler continued with his plan for the invasion and conquest of central Europe.

APPEASEMENT: 1938

British prime minister Neville Chamberlain (1937–1940) took office in 1937. In the next year, Hitler ordered forces into the Sudetenland, a region of western Czechoslovakia with a large ethnic German population. To deal with the crisis, Chamberlain favored negotiations over the use of threats or outright military force. At a meeting with Hitler in the German city of Munich in late September, British and French leaders conceded German control of the Sudetenland, despite the protests of the Czech government. Returning home, Chamberlain proudly held up the Munich Agreement and promised the British a new era of peace and cooperation with Nazi Germany. In a speech to the British parliament, the prime minister declared:

> The peoples of the British Empire were at one with those of Germany, of France and of Italy, and their anxiety, their intense desire for peace, pervaded the whole atmosphere of the conference. . . . The path which leads to appeasement is long and bristles with obstacles. The question of Czechoslovakia is the latest and perhaps the most dangerous. Now that we have got past it, I feel that it may be possible to make further progress along the road to sanity.

Chamberlain's agreement with Hitler abruptly failed in March 1939, when Germany invaded the rest of Czechoslovakia and overthrew the Czech government. Chamberlain reinforced the British military and promised the government of Poland, the next target of Hitler's threats, military support in the case of a German invasion. When Hitler followed through on his threats to attack Poland on September 1, 1939, Britain and France declared war on Germany, setting off World War II in Europe.

See also: Britain; Kellogg-Briand Pact; League of Nations; Treaty of Versailles (1919); World War II.

FURTHER READING

McDonough, Frank. *Hitler, Chamberlain, and Appeasement.* New York: Cambridge University Press, 2002.

Neville, Peter. *Hitler and Appeasement: The British Attempt to Prevent the Second World War.* Hambledon & London, 2007.

Self, Robert C. *Neville Chamberlain: A Biography.* Farnham, England: Ashgate Publishing, 2007.

Axis Powers

Alliance of three major powers formed in the 1930s, and which fought against the **Allies** during World War II (1939–1945). The term *Rome-Berlin axis* was used by the Italian dictator Benito Mussolini (r. 1922–1943) after his nation signed a military pact with Germany in October 1936. Mussolini had in mind an alliance of Europe's dictatorial **Fascist** nations. He believed these nations would play a central role in world history. **Isolationists** within the United States saw the Axis powers as representing a modern political movement, and not as a direct military threat.

GERMAN EXPANSION

Germany, the strongest of the Axis powers, had been expanding the territory under its direct control since 1938, when it **annexed** Austria and invaded the Sudetenland region of Czechoslovakia. The League of Nations could not stop German or Italian aggression with threats or economic **sanctions**. Germany had already renounced the Treaty of Versailles in 1935, and Mussolini did not bow to economic pressure from Great Britain or France, countries still unwilling to oppose the Axis with military force.

JAPANESE AGGRESSION

The Japanese government was dominated by a class of military officers who sought to aggressively expand Japanese influence in Asia. Japan's invasion of Manchuria in northern China was condemned by the League of Nations, and Japan believed its interests aligned with those of Germany and Italy. In 1935, Japan and Germany signed the Anti-Comintern Pact, in which the two nations agreed to mutual aid in case of war with the Soviet Union.

Axis Powers in World War II	
Major Powers	**Minor Powers**
Germany	Hungary
Italy	Bulgaria
Japan	Romania
	Yugoslavia

THE TRIPARTITE PACT

After invading and occupying the rest of Czechoslovakia, the German dictator Adolf Hitler (1933–1945) declared his intention to seek *lebensraum* ("living space") in eastern Europe. He ordered the invasion of Poland on September 1, 1939. This brought a declaration of war from the governments of Britain and France, touching off World War II. On September 27, 1940, Germany, Italy, and Japan signed the Tripartite Pact, establishing a formal alliance among the Axis powers. The Axis would later be joined by smaller nations including Hungary, Romania, and Bulgaria.

In southeastern Europe, Italy invaded Albania, a small Balkan country, and then North Africa. In Asia, the Japanese government announced the founding of the Greater East Asia Co-Prosperity Sphere, an alliance of nations to be controlled by the Japanese government. To this end, Japan attacked many regions of Southeast Asia and several islands in the western Pacific Ocean. Japanese aggression was met by an economic **boycott** by the United States. Although Great Britain was under heavy air assault by the German air force, and France was invaded and occupied in the spring of 1940, a strong current of isolationism still prevented the President Franklin D. Roosevelt (1933–1945) for asking Congress to declare war on the Axis.

Seeing a conflict with the United States as inevitable, Japanese military leaders prepared a surprise attack that would cripple the U.S. Navy before the war could begin. A Japanese force, made up of aircraft carriers, midget submarines, and hundreds of low-altitude bombers, attacked the U.S. military base at Pearl Harbor, Hawaii, on December 7, 1941. The attack was met with a declaration of war by the U.S. Congress, bringing the United States into the war against the Axis.

AXIS RETREATS

By the time of the attacks on Pearl Harbor, the Axis armies were advancing on three continents. The Axis reached its greatest extent in 1942. That summer, German armies were fighting on the outskirts of Moscow, the capital of the Soviet Union, and advancing as far east as the Volga River. The following winter, however, the defeat of the German army at Stalingrad on the banks of the Volga in southern Russia turned the tide of the war in Europe. German armies were gradually forced back on the eastern front. On June 6, 1944, the Allies invaded northern France and succeeded in pushing the German armies east, across the Rhine River and back into Germany proper.

In the meantime, Benito Mussolini was ousted from power. In September 1943, the Italian government signed a separate peace with the Allies. In April 1945, Mussolini was captured by pro-Allied **partisans** and executed. In the same month, the German capital of Berlin fell to the Allies. Adolf Hitler committed suicide in a fortified underground bunker in the center of Berlin. One week later, Germany surrendered.

WAR IN THE PACIFIC

For the last undefeated Axis power, the war continued in the Pacific region. U.S. air and naval forces moved westward across the island chains of the western Pacific, destroying Japanese strongholds in the Marshall Islands, the Philippines, and Okinawa. In August 1945, the United States dropped atomic bombs on Hiroshima and Nagasaki, two important cities on the Japanese mainland. This attack convinced the Japanese government to formally surrender in September 1945. After the Allied victory in World War II, the United States abandoned its isolationist foreign policy.

See also: Hitler, Adolf; Italy; Japan; Mussolini, Benito; World War II.

FURTHER READING

Adams, Simon. *World War II*. New York: DK Children, 2007.

Dinardo, R. L. *Germany and the Axis Powers: From Coalition to Collapse*. Lawrence: University Press of Kansas, 2005.

Taylor, A. J. P. *The Origins of the Second World War*. New York: Simon and Schuster, 1996.

B–D

Borah, William E. (1865–1940)

Known as The Lion of Idaho, a U.S. senator who was crucial in keeping the country out of the League of Nations, thus reinforcing the policy of isolationism after World War I (1914–1918). He was considered one of the most powerful senators of his time and became zealous when it came to questions of morality.

EARLY CAREER

His first run for political office was for a senate seat in 1903, but he lost the election. Borah ran again in 1907 and won the seat, a position he would hold until his death. Borah was a staunch **isolationist** from the time

Senator William E. Borah (left), a well-known isolationist, confers with other U.S. senators during a 1924 corruption investigation of members of President Warren Harding's cabinet.

he arrived in the Senate, and this sentiment greatly influenced U.S. foreign policy throughout his tenure.

A STUBBORN INDEPENDENCE

Borah was noted for maintaining an independent streak. Although he was a **progressive** Republican, he would not follow the party line. Even after it became clear that the Republican Party was the less progressive party, Borah refused to join the Democrats, instead choosing to be an example of what he believed a Republican *should* be.

In 1919, after the end of World War I, Borah became one of the **"Irreconcilables"** in the Senate; he would not vote to ratify the Treaty of Versailles and join the League of Nations. Borah believed that the United States had risen to its place of prominence in the world by keeping out of foreign and European affairs. His political philosophy was to fear centralized power. He believed the League of Nations would have given foreign governments a say in American affairs by requiring the nation to defend other counties, thereby removing power from individual citizens even more than the federal government had already done.

In 1919, while President Woodrow Wilson (1913–1921) traveled the country giving speeches in support of the treaty, Borah traveled the country giving speeches opposing it. One of Borah's most memorable speeches was given on November 19, 1919, on the floor of the Senate against the League of Nations. His persuasiveness contributed to the defeat of the treaty.

BORAH AND THE NEW DEAL

In 1933, when President Franklin D. Roosevelt (1933–1945) presented Congress with programs known as the **New Deal**, Borah took his time examining each bill to decide which he would support. Rather than throwing his lot in with Roosevelt and approving whatever the president wanted, he evaluated each proposal based on his principles. Borah was considered unpredictable and unknowable, basing his influence on his power and eloquence as a speaker.

Toward the end of Borah's life, it became clear that another world war was mounting. Borah's stance on the German takeover of Europe left many people with the impression that he was naive when it came to international politics. Further tarnishing his reputation, he made complimentary statements about Nazi dictator Adolf Hitler (r. 1933–1945), comparing him to Charlemagne, the great emperor of the Franks in the 700s. Failing to see the evil ideology of the Nazis, Borah is quoted as having said that if Hitler could have "only moderate[d] his religious and racial intolerance," he could have been a great world leader. Borah even believed that he could have stopped World War II (1939–1945) if he could have had a chance to speak with Hitler in person.

Borah did not live to see the United States break its isolationist stance and join World War II. He died on January 20, 1940. The United States did not enter World War II until December 1941.

See also: Hitler, Adolf; League of Nations; Republican Party; Treaty of Versailles; Wilson, Woodrow; World War I; World War II.

FURTHER READING

Ashby, Leroy. *The Spearless Leader: Senator Borah & the Progressive Movement in the 1920s.* Champaign: University of Illinois Press, 1972.

Central Powers

In Central Europe, an alliance of states that opposed the **Allies** of France, Great Britain, Russia, and later the United States during World War I (1914–1918). The Central powers included Germany, Austria-Hungary, the Ottoman Empire, and Bulgaria. In the view of U.S. **isolationists**, this complex web of European alliances made military conflict more likely and threatened to draw the United States into a fruitless and damaging war.

Central Powers in World War I	
Major Powers	Minor Powers
Germany Austria-Hungary Ottoman Empire	Bulgaria

Paul von Hindenburg (left), Kaiser Wilhelm II (center), and Erich von Ludendorff (right), three leaders of the German Empire, discuss war plans during World War I. Despite its superior numbers and firepower, the German army was unable to break through French lines during the summer offensive of 1914, which began the war. The result was four years of murderous trench warfare that ended with Germany's defeat.

In 1871, the Franco-Prussian War (1870–1871) had ended with the defeat of France by the armies of Prussia, a kingdom in northeastern Germany. The unification of the German Empire during this period gave rise to a centralized German government, with its capital in Berlin, the largest Prussian city. Seeking to form a defensive alliance against France and its ally Russia, Germany signed a pact with Austria-Hungary in 1879. Italy joined this pact in 1882, creating the Triple Alliance.

At the turn of the century, the governments of Great Britain, France, and Russia sought a balance of power in Europe by forming an alliance of their own, known as the Triple Entente. Each power pledged to support the other in case of an attack by a member of the Triple Alliance.

WORLD WAR I

At this time, political turmoil in the Balkan Peninsula was gradually drawing the two alliances—the Entente and the Triple Alliance—into conflict. The declining Ottoman Empire was challenged by Austria-Hungary for control of the Balkan region. Rising **nationalism**, or intense devotion to one's nation, among the Serbs and other ethnic groups sparked a series of wars involving the Ottoman Empire and smaller states. In 1914, a Serbian nationalist assassinated Archduke Franz Ferdinand, heir to the Austrian throne. With the support of Germany, Austria retaliated, while the Serbs called on their ally, Russia, for assistance. The tangle of treaties and alliances quickly brought France, Great Britain, and Germany into conflict by the end of the summer. Germany's invasion of Belgium in August 1914 began World War I.

War! Citing the defensive nature of the Triple Alliance, the Italian government refused to join Germany and Austria in direct military action against the Triple Entente. Italy joined the Entente in spring 1915. In the meantime, armies of the Ottoman Empire clashed with Russian forces in the Balkan Peninsula, which prompted the Ottoman government to join the Central powers. Seeing an opportunity to gain territory at the expense of its neighbors in the region, Bulgaria joined the Central powers as well.

A Long Fight The war dragged on for four years, with neither side gaining a significant advantage. In spring 1917, the United States joined the war on the side of the Allies. On the eastern front, a **Communist** government took power in Russia, signing a separate peace with Germany in early 1918. Later that year, however, an Allied **offensive** forced the German armies to retreat. In the Balkans, Bulgaria also found itself on the defensive. Bulgaria, the Ottoman Empire, and Austria all signed **armistices** with the Allies. The fall of the Austrian and Ottoman empires ended their alliance with the Central powers. On the western front, Germany asked for an armistice to end the fighting in November. Peace in Europe was made official by the Treaty of Versailles, signed in June 1919. After the war ended, however, the United States returned to its isolationist foreign policy.

See also: France; Great Britain; Treaty of Versailles (1919); World War I.

FURTHER READING
Fromkin, David. *Europe's Last Summer: Who Started the Great War in 1914?* New York: Vintage, 2005.
Keegan, John. *The First World War.* New York: Vintage, 2000.
Martel, Gordon. *Origins of the First World War.* Revised Third Edition. Longman, 2008.

Chamberlain, Neville

See Appeasement, Policy of.

Communism

See Russian Revolution and Civil War.

Coolidge, Calvin (1872–1933)

Thirtieth president of the United States, a leader who embodied traditional **conservative** values and restored the public's confidence in the presidency in the mid- to late 1920s. Calvin Coolidge pursued a foreign policy based on isolationism.

EARLY CAREER
Coolidge entered Amherst College in 1891 and graduated in 1895. By 1897,

he had passed the bar exam in Massachusetts. In 1898, Coolidge opened his own law office in Northampton, Massachusetts. He was not a trial lawyer but a transactional lawyer, meaning he drew up documents for businesses. Coolidge got a reputation among local businesses as a hard worker.

MOVE INTO POLITICS

In 1898, the same year he opened his law office, Coolidge was elected to the Northampton, Massachusetts, city council, launching his political career. He became chairman of the Northampton Republican Committee in 1904 and was elected mayor of Northampton in 1909. In 1911, Coolidge became a Massachusetts state senator. After one term, he became lieutenant governor in 1915.

Coolidge entered the national political stage after being elected governor of Massachusetts in 1918. The Boston police had formed a union and gone on strike. To quiet the riots that followed, Coolidge called out the state guard. Many of the Boston police were fired for their role in the strike, and Coolidge supported this measure. He is quoted as saying, "There is no right to strike against the public safety by anybody, anywhere, any time."

This stance against the power of the labor unions made Coolidge popular in the Republican Party, and it nominated him as Warren G. Harding's running mate in the 1920 presidential election. Like Harding, Coolidge was an old-style Republican. He did not side with the **progressive** Republicans, who had aligned themselves with Theodore Roosevelt and his Bull Moose Party.

THE HARDING-COOLIDGE ADMINISTRATIONS

Harding and Coolidge won the election of 1920 handily. At the time, the vice presidency carried few responsibilities. Coolidge became the first vice president to sit in on cabinet meetings, but he did not seem to have much influence on policy. On August 2, 1923, President Harding unexpectedly died. Coolidge was sworn in as president by his father, a notary public, in the family's home in Vermont at 2:47 A.M. on August 3.

Scandals Reports of scandal and corruption had just emerged concerning Harding's administration, and it fell to Coolidge to "clean house." He rooted out the corrupt officials and restored public confidence in the executive branch. In 1924, he was elected president in his own right.

Policy Toward Business Coolidge's main concern was making the United States a safe place for business. This meant keeping the government out of the way, an economic policy known as **laissez-faire**. Regulatory agencies were reorganized to assist businesses rather than oversee their practices. The administration believed that tax cuts to the wealthy would encourage investment in business and create a willing market in which new enterprises could grow. This, in turn, would create jobs and spread the wealth. The administration also lowered taxes overall.

Policy Toward Immigration The Immigration Act of 1924 was among the legislation passed during the Coolidge administration. This law instituted a national origins **quota** for immigrants. Each year, the same percentage of the number of immigrants already in the United States from any country would be applied to the figure of 150,000. The resulting number was how many immigrants from that country of origin would be allowed to enter.

Foreign Policy Coolidge's administration did little new in the way of foreign policy. He continued to keep the United States out of the League of Nations, thus preserving the **isolationist** foreign policy of the nation. Two members of Coolidge's administration did participate in international politics, though, winning Nobel Peace Prizes. Vice President Charles Dawes devised a program to help Germany pay its war debts for World War I (1914–1918). Secretary of State Frank Kellogg negotiated the Kellogg-Briand Pact, an agreement signed by most countries in the world renouncing the use of war as a tool of foreign policy.

See also: Dawes Plan; Harding, Warren G.; Kellogg-Briand Pact; Republican Party.

FURTHER READING
Sobel, Richard. *Coolidge*. Washington, D.C.: Regnery Publishing, 2000.
Coolidge, Calvin, and Peter Hannaford. *The Quotable Calvin Coolidge: Sensible Words for a New Century*. Bennington, Vt.: Images from the Past, 2001.

Dawes Plan

Named for Charles Dawes, a U.S. businessman and vice president under Calvin Coolidge, the Dawes Plan was a strategy that sought to reschedule the war **reparations** owed by Germany after its defeat in World War I (1914–1918). The plan was an unsuccessful attempt to intervene in German affairs at a time when most Americans favored an **isolationist** foreign policy.

TROUBLE IN GERMANY
Under the terms of the Treaty of Versailles, Germany was to pay 269 billion gold marks (the German currency), equal at the time to about $32 billion, as war reparations. The payments proved to be a heavy burden on the German government and economy. Its government treasury emptied, Germany could not pay its civil servants or make public investments. In 1923, Germany stopped making reparations payments. In retaliation, armies from France and Belgium occupied the Ruhr region of western Germany, the industrial heart of the country. The hostile armed occupation and labor unrest further strained the German economy. The German currency collapsed, **hyperinflation** drove prices steadily higher, and unemployment skyrocketed.

DAWES'S EXPERIENCE
Charles Dawes had served with the American Expeditionary Force in Europe during World War I. He was named head of the U.S. Bureau of the Budget in 1921. In 1923, he was appointed to the Allied Reparations Commission to oversee Germany's payments. In 1924, he was elected vice president on the Republican ticket with Calvin Coolidge.

In that year, Dawes formed a committee of 10 members to study the reparations problem and devise a solution. In August 1924, the committee finalized the Dawes Plan. The plan ended the occupation of the Ruhr, reorganized the German central bank, and set a new schedule of reparations payments, which began at one billion marks a year. Loans from the United States would help the German government to resume the payments.

IMPLEMENTATION OF THE PLAN

The German government agreed to the Dawes Plan. A new rentenmark replaced the now-worthless reichsmark as the German currency (one trillion old reichsmarks were exchanged for each new rentenmark). The plan was supported by **internationalists** in the U.S. government. This group wanted continued involvement in European affairs, despite the rejection of the Versailles Treaty and of the League of Nations by the Senate.

Although hyperinflation in Germany ended, and American loans allowed new investment in German industry, the heavy payments continued to burden the country with enormous debts. The crash of the U.S. stock market in late 1929 deepened the economic crisis in Germany. It soon became apparent that the German government would again be unable to maintain its scheduled payments. In 1929, the Dawes Plan was abandoned and the Young Plan came into effect, setting a timetable of 58 years for repayment of the outstanding debt of more than $26 billion.

LINKED ECONOMIES AND DEPRESSION

By making the reparations dependent on American loans, the Dawes Plan closely linked the economies of the United States and Europe. This intensified the effects of the stock market crash of 1929. The long-standing economic **depression** in Germany smoothed the path to power of Adolf Hitler (1933–1945) and the Nazi Party, ultimately leading to World War II (1939–1945). The entrance of the United States into the war in 1941 finally ended the nation's isolationist foreign policy.

See also: Treaty of Versailles (1919); War Reparations; World War I; Young Plan.

FURTHER READING

Goldstein, Erik. *The First World War Peace Settlements, 1919–1925.* Longman, 2002.

Henig, Ruth. *Versailles and After: 1919–1933.* New York: Routledge, 1995.

Kent, Bruce. *The Spoils of War: The Politics, Economics, and Diplomacy of Reparations, 1918–1932.* New York: Oxford University Press, 1992.

Democratic Party

Founded in 1828, and still in existence today, the oldest political organization in the United States and one of the nation's major political parties. In the early twentieth century, the Democratic Party was a driving force behind the abandonment of **isolationist** policy.

EARLY TWENTIETH CENTURY

After the hardships of World War I (1914–1918), the Democratic Party supported international cooperation as a tool for preventing future conflicts, while the rival Republicans were associated with isolationism, namely, avoiding world affairs. At the war's end, Democrat Woodrow Wilson (1913–1921) urged Congress and the nation to maintain an **internationalist** policy by signing the Treaty of Versailles and joining the League of Nations, but Republicans in the U.S. Senate rejected both initiatives.

After a series of Republican presidents—and the worst economic crisis in history, the **Great Depression**—Democrat Franklin D. Roosevelt (1933–1945) in 1932 won the White House in a landslide victory. Roosevelt butted heads with Republicans in Congress over how to deal with the growing threat of mounting aggression in Europe and the Pacific. Initially cooperative, the president allowed the passage of several neutrality acts in the late 1930s.

HISTORY MAKERS

Franklin D. Roosevelt (1882–1945)

Often referred to by the initials FDR, Franklin Delano Roosevelt (1933–1945) was the 32nd president of the United States and the only president to serve more than two terms in office. Known for his confidence and positive spirit, Roosevelt was the guiding force for a nation torn apart by economic decline and war.

In 1910, Roosevelt was elected to the state senate of New York and became prominent as a reformer, opposing the corrupt Tammany Hall political machine that controlled Democratic politics in the state at that time. In 1913, President Woodrow Wilson (1913–1921) appointed him assistant secretary of the navy. In 1921, a year after resigning his post, Roosevelt contracted polio, which resulted in his paralysis from the waist down. Fearing his handicap would keep him from further pursuing public office, he taught himself to walk with leg braces and insisted upon not appearing in public in a wheelchair.

Roosevelt was elected governor of New York in 1929, and in 1932, he was elected to the presidency, defeating the Republican **incumbent** Herbert Hoover (1929–1933) by more than 7 million votes. As president, he worked to pull the United States out of the Great Depression with a sometimes controversial **New Deal**—a series of laws designed to stimulate the economy and create jobs. He established regulatory agencies such as the Federal Deposit Insurance Corporation (FDIC) and Securities and Exchange Commission (SEC). He also created social programs and services, such as Social Security, that still exist today.

Roosevelt also steered the United States through World War II (1939–1945), ending the nation's isolationist stance first by aiding Great Britain in its fight against Nazi Germany and then by joining the war outright after the 1941 attack on Pearl Harbor by Japanese forces.

In 1944, Roosevelt was elected to an unprecedented fourth term, although he died a few months after his **inauguration** and before the war's end. His legacy looms large in American politics, both for his domestic and foreign policies.

However, the bombing of Pearl Harbor in Hawaii on December 7, 1941, officially ended the isolationist policies of the 1920s and 1930s. Roosevelt's insistence on the United States' inclusion in world affairs became a signature of the Democratic Party—as did his establishment of social and regulatory programs that still exist today.

See also: Fourteen Points; Treaty of Versailles; Republican Party; Wilson, Woodrow; World War I; World War II.

FURTHER READING

Schulman, Bruce J., ed. *Student's Guide to Elections*. Washington, D.C.: CQ Press, 2008.

Wagner, Heather Lehr. *The History of the Democratic Party*. New York: Chelsea House Publications, 2007.

Witcover, Jules. *Party of the People: A History of the Democrats*. New York: Random House, 2003.

E–H

Emergency Quota Act (1921)

Federal law passed to slow the influx of **immigrants** by limiting the number of immigrants arriving from each foreign nation. The law reinforced the nation's **isolationist** foreign policy by restraining influence from foreign peoples, who would naturally have some allegiance to their homelands.

EARLY IMMIGRATION

A wave of immigration brought more than 20 million immigrants into the country from eastern and southern Europe between 1875 and 1920. At the same time, the nation went through a period of rapid **industrialization**. New factories operated in large cities of the East and the Midwest, manufacturing steel, chemicals, transportation equipment, automobiles, and machinery. Drawn by the prospects for steady and well-paid jobs, immigrants filled urban neighborhoods in Boston, New York, Chicago, and other major cities.

The sharp rise in immigration that began in the late nineteenth century was interrupted by World War I (1914–1918), which prevented passenger ships from operating safely on the open seas. By 1920, the foreign-born population of the United States had reached almost 14 million out of a total of 105 million people. This was one of the highest levels of foreign-born residents in the nation's history, sparking a debate over the best way to slow the rising tide of foreign-born residents.

URBAN ISSUES AND IMMIGRATION

Many people believed the cities of the eastern United States were being overrun with "undesirable" immigrants from poor nations in southern and eastern Europe. Rising crime, delinquency, poverty, contagious disease, unemployment, and **socialism** were all blamed on the newcomers. Racist groups such as the Ku Klux Klan (KKK) made the dangers of unrestricted immigration a center of their policy and recruited new members with the promise to combat immigrants and return the country to an era of "100 percent Americanism."

Heeding anti-immigrant public opinion during the war, the U.S. Congress passed the Immigration Act of 1917—over the **veto** of President Woodrow Wilson (1913–1921). This law prevented the immigration of certain undesirables, including **anarchists**, polygamists, the illiterate, alcoholics, and criminals. After the war's end in 1918, the Red Scare—a sweeping fear of **communist** influence—and a devastating influenza epidemic intensified the public's fear of the consequences of a new wave of immigrants from war-torn Europe. The law of 1921 further limited immigrants by their country of origin. The total from each nation was limited to 3 percent of the total living in the United States in 1910, as measured by the national **census** of that year. There were no limits placed on immigration from Latin America, while all immigrants from Asia were banned. Over the next three years, the law roughly evened the number of arrivals from northern Europe vs. southern Europe and all other nations. The law, however, would be replaced in 1924 by another federal immigration law that would further limit the number of immigrants from Europe and Asia.

LATER LAWS

The Emergency Quota Act was the first to establish national **quotas**, a system that survives to this day. It was also the first to impose limits on the number of immigrants from European countries (the United States had specifically excluded Chinese immigrants by the Chinese Exclusion Act of 1882). The quotas were limited further by the Immigration Act of 1924, also known as the Johnson-Reed Act, which used the census of 1890 and lowered the number of new immigrants to 2 percent of each nationality. All these laws were attempts to keep the immigrant population of the United States low and thus help keep the nation removed from the affairs of other countries.

See also: Ku Klux Klan; National Origins Act (1924).

FURTHER READING

Craats, Rennay. *History of the 1920s.* New York: Weigl Publishers, 2001.

Daniels, Roger. *Coming to America: A History of Immigration and Ethnicity in American Life.* Second Edition. New York: Harper Perennial, 2002.

Fascism

See Mussolini, Benito.

Fordney-McCumber Act

See Republican Party; Smoot-Hawley Tariff.

Fourteen Points

Set of principles advanced by President Woodrow Wilson (1913–1921) to press his case for self-determination, **democracy**, **disarmament**, and free trade in the peace negotiations following World War I (1914–1918). After the negotiations resulted in the Treaty of Versailles, however, Wilsonian principles and the Fourteen Points came up against strong, and successful, opposition by **isolationists** in the U.S. Senate.

IDEALISTIC GOALS

Wilson revealed the Fourteen Points before a joint session of Congress on January 8, 1918. He had led the United States into the war in April 1917, a decision that resolved a long debate over the wisdom of U.S. involvement. After American troops began fighting with the **Allies** against Germany, a group of 150 scholars, known informally as the Inquiry, met over several months. The Inquiry's task was to propose a series of aims, to be reviewed by President Wilson, for the expected victory and the peace to follow.

Open Negotiations In their final form, the Fourteen Points had both abstract and specific goals. The first point was for "open negotiations, openly arrived at"—an answer to the secret treaties and agreements that many blamed for the outbreak of the war in 1914. The following points supported freedom of navigation, free trade, the reduction of armaments, and the fair settling of disputed borders.

An Association of Nations These first principles were followed by more specific language on political and territorial issues in France, Russia, Italy, Austria-Hungary, Serbia and the Balkan region, Poland, and the Ottoman Empire. The 14th and final point—the one most important to Wilson—called for the formation of an international diplomatic "association of nations," which would settle disputes among its members before they resorted to war.

NEGOTIATIONS IN PARIS

In summer 1918, Allied forces began forcing the retreat of the German army from northern France. On the belief that the Fourteen Points would guide the negotiations to come, German diplomats agreed to an **armistice** on November 11. In the next months, Wilson and his staff sailed for Europe and the Paris Peace Conference, which convened in January 1919.

Wilson found himself idolized by the public as the savior of Europe. He was greeted by the people as a celebrity. His Fourteen Points were quickly forgotten, however, as each nation negotiated for its own military, political, and economic advantage. The British held to their authority over subject peoples in Ireland and India; Italy sought to extend its control over the port of Fiume on the Adriatic Sea. For the damages it had suffered at the hands of the German army, France claimed a buffer province in Alsace-Lorraine, a territory with a German ethnic majority. German diplomats, meanwhile, were locked out of the negotiations and given no say in the terms of the final agreements.

The result was the Treaty of Versailles, signed on June 28, 1919. Although Wilson realized that the treaty ignored many of the principles

History Speaks

Wilson's Plan for International Cooperation

President Woodrow Wilson (1913–1921) first pronounced the Fourteen Points before a joint session of Congress in January 1918, while American troops were fighting in northern France. The points presented Wilson's ambitious and hopeful principles for future relations among the nations.

1. Open covenants of peace, after which there shall be no private international understandings...

2. Absolute freedom of navigation upon the seas...

3. The removal...of all economic barriers and the establishment of equality of trade conditions...

4. Adequate guarantees given and taken that national armaments will be reduced to the lowest point...

5. A free...and absolutely impartial adjustment of all colonial claims...

6. The...settlement of all questions affecting Russia...

7. Belgium, the whole world will agree, must be evacuated and restored....

8. All French territory should be freed and the invaded portions restored....

9. A readjustment of the frontiers of Italy should be effected along clearly recognizable lines of nationality.

10. The peoples of Austria-Hungary...should be accorded the freest opportunity to autonomous development.

11. Romania, Serbia, and Montenegro should be evacuated; occupied territories restored; Serbia accorded free and secure access to the sea; and the relations of the several Balkan states to one another determined by friendly counsel...

12. The Turkish portion of the present Ottoman Empire should be assured a secure sovereignty, but the other nationalities which are now under Turkish rule should be assured an undoubted security of life....

13. An independent Polish state should be erected....

14. A general association of nations must be formed under specific covenants for the purpose of affording mutual guarantees of political independence and territorial integrity....

of the Fourteen Points, he believed it was the best agreement possible under the circumstances and brought it home to the U.S. Senate for **ratification**. He believed that through the proposed League of Nations, the United States could help lead the world to an era of democracy and peace and overcome the treaty's many shortcomings.

THE IRRECONCILABLES

In Washington, Wilson found a strong faction of the Republican Party, led by William Borah of Idaho and Henry Cabot Lodge of Massachusetts, opposing the treaty and the League of Nations. The opposition was divided into three factions: While the "strong reservationists" demanded a complete renegotiation of the treaty, the "mild reservationists" wanted some **amendments** to the treaty but accepted it in principle. "Irreconcilables" opposed the treaty as well as the league in any form. **Nativists** within this faction believed the United States should avoid any more foreign entanglements, such as the disastrous war that had just ended, and pointed to Article X of the charter of the League of Nations as evidence that the country would be promising just that:

> The members of the League undertake to respect and preserve as against external aggression the territorial integrity and existing political independence of all Members of the League. In case of any such aggression or in case of any threat or danger of such aggression the Council shall advise upon the means by which this obligation shall be fulfilled.

Article XI also caused concern among some members of the Senate:

> Any war or threat of war, whether immediately affecting any of the Members of the League or not, is hereby declared a matter of concern to the whole League, and the League shall take any action that may be deemed wise and effectual to safeguard the peace of nations.

Isolationist Views The opposing factions saw the treaty as a threat to the **sovereignty** of the United States. Article X, specifically, imposed a heavy obligation to intervene whenever problems arose among any of the member nations, which were spread around the globe. The threat of this happening was greater since the United States had emerged during the war as a military power, with an air force and navy now equal to those of Great Britain and able to project American power across the seas.

Instead of submitting to the commitments of such a league, said Lodge and his allies in the Senate, the United States would do better to keep within its borders and stay out of conflicts, in Europe and elsewhere, in which it had no pressing political or economic interest. This isolationist sentiment found strong support among the American public, weary of war and mindful of Europe's violent history.

Domestic Issues Postwar domestic turmoil also worked against the treaty. The United States was experiencing a slowing economy, high unemployment, labor conflict, and the "Red Scare," during which the authorities arrested and deported hundreds of suspected **communists**. The public took little interest in international diplomacy or Wilsonian ideals of a just and lasting peace.

As head of the Senate Committee on Foreign Affairs, Lodge craftily used Wilson's own stubbornness and refusal to compromise against ratification of the treaty in the Senate. He first read out the entire treaty in the Senate chamber, word for word. He then called witnesses to testify against its passage. In mocking imitation of the Fourteen Points, Lodge announced the "fourteen reservations," amendments to the treaty's terms that would allow it to win passage in the Senate.

A STUBBORN PRESIDENT

Wilson refused to compromise or change any part of the treaty, insisting that it pass in its original form or not at all. To counter the growing opposition, Wilson undertook a difficult whistle-stop tour of the Midwest and the West, speaking from a railroad car on the virtues of the Fourteen Points and the League of Nations, and insisting that the United States had a moral obligation to help keep the international peace. Having emerged from the war as a military power, the country now had to accept the responsibilities that went with that power.

Wilson's tour, which ended in September after the president suffered a paralyzing stroke, did nothing to turn back anti-treaty sentiment in the Senate or to blunt the arguments of Borah, Lodge, and other isolationists. On November 19, 1919, the final day of debate, Borah delivered a rousing speech in which he rejected the treaty and its "entangling alliances," even with the reservations added to it by Lodge. With Lodge's reservations, the treaty was rejected by a vote of 53 to 38. The reservations were then stripped out, which led to another rejection by a vote of 53 to 38 on January 19, 1920. Needing a two-thirds majority to pass, the treaty failed for the third and final time on March 19, 1920. The failure of the treaty reinforced the trend to isolationism in the United States, a trend that would gain strength through the 1920s and 1930s.

See also: Borah, William E.; League of Nations; Lodge, Henry Cabot; Republican Party; Treaty of Versailles (1919); Wilson, Woodrow; World War I.

FURTHER READING
Knock, Thomas J. *To End All Wars: Woodrow Wilson and the Quest for a New World Order.* Princeton, N.J.: Princeton University Press, 1995.
Lodge, Henry Cabot. *The Senate and the League of Nations.* New York: Charles Scribner's Sons, 1925.
Macmillan, Margaret. *Paris 1919.* New York: Random House, 2001.
Streissguth, Tom. *Eyewitness History: The Roaring Twenties.* Revised Edition. New York: Facts On File, 2007.

France

Nation in western Europe and a member of the **Allies** that defeated the Central Powers in World War I (1914–1918). American participation in World War I strengthened the feelings of isolationism in the United States after the war.

By 1918, the French and other Allied powers had beat the Germans and gained a sense that the future of Europe lay with them. The people of France enthusiastically supported President Woodrow Wilson's (1913–1921) effort to create a lasting peace through a League of Nations, while French prime minister Georges Clemenceau sought to impose the harshest possible conditions on Germany in the Treaty of Versailles. The French hoped that the huge **reparations** due from Germany, and the strict limits on the German military, would prevent another war.

AFTER WORLD WAR I

After the war, the French economy went through a difficult adjustment. The franc, the French currency, lost much of its value, and the price of basic goods and food rose sharply. The loss of more than 2 million dead and wounded in World War I decimated the workforce. France protected its industries and agriculture with high **tariffs** on imported goods. When the economic **depression** hit France, its effects lasted longer than in Great Britain and the United States, leading to greater political and social turmoil.

During World War I, France had suffered the destruction of vast swaths of productive land in the north. Hoping to prevent another German invasion, the French military built a line of earthworks, walls, and fortifications, known as the Maginot Line. However, the Maginot Line was built with massed infantry battles in mind. It would do nothing to prevent air attacks or long-range artillery bombardments. In addition, the Maginot Line stopped at France's border with Belgium, where Germany had attacked in 1914. Instead of preventing another German attack, the Maginot Line provided a false sense of security while the French neglected to produce needed artillery, tanks, and aircraft.

NEW FEARS

The fear of German aggression grew through the 1930s as the dictator Adolf Hitler (1933–1945) took control of Germany and promised to revive the country's military might. Hitler reoccupied the industrial Rhineland, in violation of the Treaty of Versailles, and rebuilt the German military. Under Prime Minister Aristide Briand, France tried a policy of appeasement toward Germany, hoping to avoid another war. The French government knew well that Germany still outnumbered France in population and had much greater industrial capacity. In addition, a sharp drop in the birth rate during World War I made far fewer men available for **conscription** during the late 1930s.

The French government did not want to risk a confrontation with Hitler. As a result, France did nothing to challenge Hitler's occupation of the Rhineland or the German unification with Austria, both of which violated the Treaty of Versailles. French diplomats also went along with British prime minister Neville Chamberlain's policy of appeasement and the Munich Agreement of 1938, in which western Czechoslovakia was surrendered to Germany. A military alliance was struck with Britain and with Poland. However, when Germany invaded Poland in September 1939, France found itself unable, and unwilling, to challenge Hitler with military action on a western front. The French army remained passive inside the forts of the Maginot Line.

GERMANY INVADES

In spring 1940, German tank divisions rolled across Belgium and into northern France. Paris, the French capital, fell in a matter of weeks. The military failure resulted in an occupation of France by Germany, while the United States—because of its **isolationist** foreign policy—remained **neutral** in the conflict. The efforts at appeasement of Germany, and the **nonintervention** policy of the United States, ensured that the effects of World War II (1939–1945) would be even more devastating to France and the rest of Europe.

See also: Appeasement, Policy of; Treaty of Versailles (1919); World War I; World War II.

FURTHER READING

Bloch, Marc. *Strange Defeat.* New York: W.W. Norton, 2001.

Popkin, Jeremy D. *A History of Modern France.* Third Edition. Englewood Cliffs, N.J.: Prentice-Hall, 2005.

Shirer, William. *The Collapse of the Third Republic.* New York: Da Capo Press, 1994.

Germany

See Hitler, Adolf.

Great Britain

Island nation, located off the northwestern coast of Europe and one of the Allied powers during World War I (1914–1918) that defeated Germany and the other Central Powers. The close relationship between the United States and Great Britain that developed during and after the war was key in bringing an end to the **isolationist** policies of the United States throughout the 1920s and 1930s.

During the war, British armies in France and Belgium suffered more than a million dead and wounded. Although the war against Germany ultimately ended in victory, the British economy struggled for years afterward with a lack of manpower, investment, and foreign trade. Later, in the 1930s, a **Fascist** movement sympathetic to Adolf Hitler's (1933–1945) Nazi Germany gained a large following, while riots and strikes shut down factories and mines throughout Britain, causing even more economic hardship.

For a century after American independence, Great Britain remained a rival of the United States. At the beginning of the twentieth century, many Americans still saw the British as tyrannical **monarchists**, determined only to expand and defend their far-flung colonial empire. In 1917, however, the plight of the Allies in northern France ended the age-old hostility between the United

States and Great Britain. American troops arrived at the side of the British in the trenches of northern France. The new alliance endured through the twentieth century and to the present time.

APPEASEMENT

The growing Nazi menace in Europe in the 1930s at first inspired a policy of appeasement on the part of the British government. Indeed, in 1938, Prime Minister Neville Chamberlain (1937–1940) reached an accord, the Munich Agreement, with Nazi dictator Adolf Hitler. Chamberlain promised the British a new era of peace and cooperation with Nazi Germany. With the German invasion of Poland on September 1, 1939, however, the British steeled for a German assault. British cities came under merciless attack by the German air force, and British ships faced great peril in the North Sea and the North Atlantic Ocean from German cruisers and submarines, known as U-boats.

Although he knew that the American public opposed direct involvement, President Franklin D. Roosevelt (1933–1945) methodically prepared the country for war. In December 1940, Roosevelt proposed a "Lend-Lease" program. To help the British, the United States would allow American ships and war materials to be used by the British armed forces. Isolationists opposed the program as a defense of British **imperialism** and a deliberate step toward participation in the war—which they saw as solely Europe's problem.

The U.S. Congress passed the Lend-Lease program in March 1941.

In June, when Germany invaded the Soviet Union, the program expanded to assist the Soviet government. **Internationalists** believed the United States had a duty to help the British and the Soviets to prevent a Nazi conquest of Europe. Such an event would endanger the United States, in this view, and had to be opposed by any means possible. Supporters of Lend-Lease also believed that providing war material to the Allies would allow them, eventually, to defeat Germany on their own and make American military involvement unnecessary.

INCREASING U.S. INVOLVEMENT

As the battle of the North Atlantic raged on through 1941, German U-boat attacks on merchant shipping destroyed arms bound for Great Britain. In response, Roosevelt ordered U.S. escort vessels into the battle zone to provide convoy protection. In September, U.S. vessels were authorized to fire on German ships and submarines. To opponents of intervention, the United States was being dragged into the war without a formal declaration by Congress, which was a violation of the Constitution.

The Japanese attack on Pearl Harbor on December 7, 1941, brought the war directly to U.S. territory from a different direction—the Pacific theater. The attack ended the debate over intervention and brought the United States immediately into World War II.

See also: America First Committee; Appeasement, Policy of; France; World War I; World War II.

FURTHER READING

Churchill, Winston. *The Gathering Storm.* Mariner Books, 1986.

Marr, Andrew. *A History of Modern Britain.* London: Macmillan UK, 2008.

Harding, Warren G. (1865–1923)

Twenty-ninth president of the United States, Warren G. Harding returned the country to a state of calm following World War I (1914–1918). In the aftermath of the war, Harding's administration was committed to a policy of **isolationism**.

EARLY LIFE

In the late 1880s, Harding and a friend purchased a failing newspaper, the *Marion Daily Star*. In 1891, Harding married Florence Kling. Florence was hardworking and ambitious. She helped make the *Marion Daily Star* a successful business and urged Harding into politics. The success of the paper made him a prominent man in the community, despite a personal lack of drive.

MOVE INTO POLITICS

Harding began associating with business leaders and others with influence and power. This led him into politics and the Republican Party. It has been said of Harding that his greatest qualification for political office was that he looked like a leader. He was well dressed and handsome, so people felt that he was trustworthy and competent.

In 1899, Harding was elected to the Ohio state senate. He ran for governor in 1910 but lost. In 1914, he was elected to the U.S. Senate. His tenure as a senator was less than impressive. He missed more votes than he attended, which had the uncertain benefit of letting him avoid making enemies. Because he never expressed a strong opinion on any subject and did not vote, he did not disappoint anyone.

Despite his poor showing in the Senate, Harding was nominated for president in 1920. The presidency of Woodrow Wilson (1913–1921) had been difficult for the country. Wilson pushed a **progressive** reform agenda that put the country through internal upheaval. Additionally, the United States had been drawn into World War I. Americans were drafted, and the government cracked down on **dissent**. The prices of goods soared, as did taxes. American life changed quickly, and in 1920, the public remained war weary.

HARDING'S PRESIDENTIAL PLATFORM

Harding's platform was what he called a "return to normalcy." To a large extent, this meant reversing Wilson's progressive reforms. The United States became more **isolationist**. Harding had opposed joining the League of Nations during Wilson's presidency, and this sentiment continued. Immigration was greatly restricted. He implemented high **tariffs** to protect American business and lowered taxes.

The great failure of Harding's presidency was its rampant corruption. Harding's cabinet members took advantage of their power, reaping great profits. Harding was not personally involved in any of the scandals, but he was deeply distressed by the betrayal of his trust, which took a toll on his health. As the corruption was coming to light, Harding took a trip to Alaska. On the return journey, he died in a San Francisco hotel on August 2, 1923.

See also: Coolidge, Calvin; Republican Party; Wilson, Woodrow; World War I.

FURTHER READING

Dean, John W. *Warren G. Harding.* New York: Times Books, 2004.

McCartney, Laton. *The Teapot Dome Scandal: How Big Oil Bought the Harding White House and Tried to Steal the Country.* New York: Random House Trade Paperback, 2009.

Hitler, Adolf (1889–1945)

Leader of the Nazi Party and chancellor and führer of the Third Reich in Germany. Hitler was responsible for the European theater of World War II (1939–1945) and the deaths of at least 43 million people on all sides.

EARLY LIFE

Adolf Hitler was born on April 20, 1889, in Braunau in upper Austria. His father was a government bureaucrat, working at the nearby border crossing between Germany and Austria. He was his parents' third child, although the previous two died while infants. A younger brother also died as a child, leaving Adolf's younger sister, Paula, as his only surviving sibling.

The young Hitler was an average to poor student. He did not graduate high school, dropping out at 16. His overbearing and violent father wanted him to become a customs officer, but Adolf wanted to be an artist. He later admitted that his failures at school were an act of rebellion.

After leaving high school, Hitler moved to Vienna, Austria. His father died in 1903, and Adolf then survived on his father's pension. He tried twice to get into the Academy of Fine Arts in Vienna, but failed. He owned little, moved often, and tried to eke out a living painting postcards. Hitler's life was isolated and lonely.

In 1913, Hitler moved to Munich, Germany. When World War I (1914–1918) broke out, he volunteered to join the German army. His military service gave him purpose. He was reportedly an undisciplined soldier, but eager for action. His incredible luck saw him through the war mostly unharmed. In 1916, he was wounded in the leg and sent away from the frontlines to recover. He received two Iron Crosses for his bravery.

RISE OF ANTI-SEMITISM

Hitler's **anti-Semitism**, or hatred of the Jews, grew from a variety of sources. During the time he lived in Vienna, the city was a hotbed of radical thought. The city was, generally, racist and supported religious **prejudice**, especially against Jews. Lutheranism and the writings of Martin Luther were particularly influential. When Hitler visited Berlin during his recovery, he attributed the apathy of the Germans to Jewish influence. When Germany began to lose World War I, Hitler laid the blame for this on the "invisible foes of the German people," namely Jews and **Marxists**.

Adolf Hitler speaks at a Nazi Party rally in Dortmund, Germany, shortly after his election as chancellor of Germany in 1933. His powerful rhetoric roused a population desperate for economic recovery and determined to right the unjust terms of the Treaty of Versailles.

When Germany finally lost the war, Hitler was filled with hatred. The country he had been fighting for had been defeated. Kaiser Wilhelm II (1888–1918), the German emperor, no longer ruled the nation. Hitler did not blame the **Allies**, however. Instead, Hitler put the blame on German politicians and the secretive threat of the Jews, who he believed had conspired to bring Germany down. The humiliation of Germany in its defeat increased growing **nationalist** sentiments, which ultimately resulted in the founding and growth of the Nazi Party.

Nazi Party Hitler's anti-Jewish speeches made him popular with his military superiors. Fellow soldiers were happy to hear that they had someone to blame for their losses. In 1919, Hitler was given an assignment as an "educational officer." Effectively, his job was to be a spy, investigating political parties. He went to Munich to investigate the German Workers' Party, which he then joined. The party was renamed to *Nationalsozialistische Deutsche Arbeiterpartei*, or the Nazi Party, and Hitler began working his way up the ranks, using his skills as a speaker to advance the party's **propaganda**.

The party's influence grew. It established its own army, the SA, to protect its meetings and attack its enemies. By 1921, Hitler had taken control of the party. He used the party and its growing number of followers to try to take over the government of the German state of Bavaria and turn it against the Weimar Republic, the government of Germany. The coup failed, and Hitler was imprisoned. It was during this time that he wrote *Mein Kampf*, his **manifesto** for the Nazi Party and revitalization of Germany.

Increasing Influence After he was released from prison in 1924, Hitler started to make real strides in gaining power. Germany was going through an economic **depression**, and his rhetoric brought the German people hope. He received the support of business leaders and newspapers, which would print his propaganda. People from all classes of society wanted to hear that Germany would again be a great nation, and so Hitler's power grew. The Nazi Party was winning power legally, through elections to political office.

RISE TO SUPREME POWER
In 1933, Hitler was elected chancellor of Germany. It was a turning point for the country. Hitler suspended the constitution; had his political opponents murdered by his personal bodyguards, a military group called the SS (*Schutzstaffel*, German for "protective squadron"); and made any opposition to the Nazi regime illegal. He consolidated all political power in himself, giving himself the title of führer, or leader. Opponents of the Third Reich were sent to concentration camps or killed.

Hitler quickly began building up the German military, which had been limited to 100,000 men by the Treaty of Versailles at the end of World War I. While Britain, France, and the League of Nations condemned Germany for breaking the treaty, they believed Hitler's reassurances that Germany was not out to start a war. Convinced that Hitler was dedicated to peace, the international community did not stop the rearmament. Further undermining the Treaty of Versailles, Britain agreed to allow Germany to increase the size of its navy. This was done without the consultation or agreement from the other signers of the treaty.

In 1936, Hitler occupied an area known as the Rhineland, in direct violation of the Treaty of Versailles. The European powers did nothing, which Hitler took as encouragement that his plans for German expansion would not be opposed. Hitler then expanded German rule to Austria. He also established a treaty with Italy, which was suffering from **sanctions** by Britain and France. After **annexing** Austria, Hitler turned his sights on the Sudetenland, a German-populated area of Czechoslovakia. The Germans of Sudetenland began protesting to be allowed to leave Czechoslovakia and join with the newly enlarged German state. The other great European powers at the time, Britain and France, were unconcerned by these events, and through the appeasement policies of the 1938 Munich Agreement,

Germany annexed Sudetenland as well.

LACK OF INTERNATIONAL REACTION

Europe and the United States did little but condemn Hitler's rise in power and grab for land. Even though he claimed that Sudetenland was the only region Germany wished to annex, in March 1939, he invaded Czechoslovakia. The country was declared a **protectorate**.

When Germany launched its attack on Poland in 1939, Britain and France intervened. On September 1, the invasion began. On September 3, Britain and France declared war on Germany.

U.S. FOREIGN POLICY

Initially, the United States maintained its isolationist stance. Americans still believed that Europe's problems were its own. The United States was not part of the Treaty of Versailles ending World War I. Although it was involved in the treaty's negotiations, isolationist powers in the U.S. Senate had refused to **ratify** the treaty.

By the middle of 1940, France had been divided into German- and Italian-controlled areas. Great Britain was under attack from the German air force, or *luftwaffe*. The United States was offering money and arms to the Allies, but did not declare war. The public continued to support isolation.

The United States did commit part of its navy to protecting British ships, which effectively put them into combat with Germany, but the country remained officially **neutral**. Even after the Japanese attack on Pearl Harbor on December 7, 1941, the United States did not declare war on Germany. Congress voted to declare war on the Japanese. In response, Germany declared war on the United States, ending any chance at remaining neutral in Hitler's war.

See also: Axis Powers; France; Great Britain; Japan; League of Nations; Pearl Harbor; Treaty of Versailles; World War I; World War II.

FURTHER READING

Fuchs, Thomas. *A Concise Biography of Adolf Hitler.* New York: Berkley Books, 2000.

Ward, Geoffrey C. *The War: An Intimate History, 1941–1945.* New York: Knopf, 2007.

Immigration

See Emergency Quota Act (1921); National Origins Act (1924).

Italy

See Mussolini, Benito.

Irreconcilables

See Borah, William E.; League of Nations; Lodge, Henry Cabot.

J–L

Japan

Located off the eastern coast of Asia, an island nation that joined the allied nations of the Triple Entente during World War I (1914–1918). Although there was little fighting in Asia, the victory of the alliance helped Japan to emerge as the leading military power in the region. Later, in 1940, the militaristic government of Japan joined with Nazi Germany and **Fascist** Italy to form the Axis powers. Japan's attack on Pearl Harbor, Hawaii, on December 7, 1941, brought the United States into World War II (1939–1945) and ended the U.S. foreign policy of isolationism.

AFTER WORLD WAR I

In the years following World War I, the Japanese government came under the control of a strongly **nationalistic** officer class. The military was determined to expand Japanese territory and influence throughout Asia and the Pacific region. Japan sought to assert its power in northern Asia. It sent military forces to Russia during the Russian civil war (1917–1921) to fight against the **Bolsheviks**, who were trying to establish a Communist government there. At the end the war, specific terms of the Treaty of Versailles, known as the Shantung Clause, gave Japan a **mandate** to govern former German colonies in East Asia.

As the civilian government of Japan favored closer relations with Western countries, Japan joined the League of Nations and pledged to seek peaceful resolution of any conflict. The military, however, operated independently of civilian leaders, and the highest Japanese officers felt no obligation to follow the direction of the country's diplomats.

Japan prospered during the 1920s. The country's new industries sold to a growing international market. Without important natural resources of their own, however, the Japanese were forced to buy raw materials and fuel on the open market or seize what they could through military action and occupation.

The **Great Depression** of the 1930s crushed the Japanese economy. High **tariffs** passed by the U.S. Congress brought a decline in global trade and shut down Japan's export market. Farmers found prices for their goods falling, and many were unable to feed their families. This desperation forced rural people into the cities, which were blighted by overcrowding and unemployment. The world economic crisis was a key cause of the Japanese military aggression through the 1930s. Ishiwara Kanji, a prominent army officer, wrote that:

> It is a publicly acknowledged fact that our national situation has reached an impasse, that there is no way of solving the food, population, and other important problems, and that the only path left open to us is development of Manchuria and Mongolia.

Japan became the first nation to openly defy the League of Nations. In 1931, the army invaded the northern Chinese province of Manchuria. Japan also occupied the former German **colony** in the Shantung province. When the league demanded that Japanese forces withdraw, Japan resigned from the league. The "Manchurian Incident" demonstrated that the league was ineffective in resolving international disputes. At the same time, Japan's civilian government came under fire from military leaders, who saw representative **democracy** as weak and divisive.

U.S. REACTION

From the U.S. point of view, Japan represented a growing threat in the western Pacific region. The Japanese invasion of China touched off a storm of anti-Japanese opinion in the United States. When Japan joined the Axis powers of Germany and Italy in September 1940, the United States began a rapid buildup of naval forces in the Pacific. Public opinion in the United States remained strongly antiwar, however, as **isolationist** groups such as the America First Committee warned against any foreign entanglements.

In 1941, when the United States banned the export of petroleum, which was essential to Japan's economy, the Japanese leadership treated this move as a hostile act. Japanese military leaders favored a surprise attack to cripple U.S. naval assets. As a result, the Japanese attacked the U.S. naval base at Pearl Harbor, Hawaii, on December 7, 1941. This aggressive action brought about the entry of the United States into the war against Japan and the other Axis powers, thus ending the U.S. foreign policy of isolationism.

See also: America First Committee; Axis Powers; League of Nations; Pearl Harbor; Russian Revolution and Civil War; World War II.

FURTHER READING

Bix, Herbert. *Hirohito and the Making of Modern Japan.* New York: Harper Perennial, 2001.

Henshall, Kenneth G. *A History of Japan, Second Edition: From Stone Age to Superpower.* London: Palgrave Macmillan, 2004.

Toland, John. *The Rising Sun: The Decline and Fall of the Japanese Empire, 1936–1945.* New York: Modern Library, 2003.

Johnson-Reed Act

See National Origins Act (1924).

Kellogg-Briand Pact (1928)

Treaty that pledged the nations that signed it to renounce war as an instrument of foreign policy. It was named for the two men who created it, U.S. secretary of state Frank Kellogg and French foreign minister Aristide Briand. **Isolationists** in the United States favored the pact; they saw it as a promising means to avoid foreign wars.

After an **armistice** had ended the fighting in World War I (1914–1918), the U.S. Senate had failed to **ratify** the Treaty of Versailles. The United States still came under pressure from its allies in Europe, and from advocates of the League of Nations, to sign some sort of international peace agreement. Two scholars, Nicholas Murray Butler and James T. Shotwell, proposed an international agreement that specifically outlawed war. Their idea was taken up by Aristide Briand, the foreign minister of France, who published an "open letter" to the U.S. government in April 1927 proposing a treaty between the two nations.

U.S. REACTION

President Calvin Coolidge (1923–1929) and his secretary of state, Frank Kellogg, had strong reservations against such a treaty. They did not want the United States obligated to protect France in case of further trouble in Europe. Instead of a **bilateral** agreement between the two nations, Kellogg proposed a **multilateral** treaty. Thus, all nations would be invited to participate in the negotiations and sign the final agreement. Kellogg also wanted the treaty to specifically ban wars of aggression and not acts of self-defense.

Fifteen nations signed the Kellogg-Briand Pact in Paris on August 27, 1928: France, the United States, the United Kingdom, Ireland, Canada, Australia, New Zealand, South Africa, India, Belgium, Poland, Czechoslovakia, Germany, Italy, and Japan. The treaty set a date of July 24, 1929, to officially go into effect.

DEBATE IN THE SENATE

In the fall of 1928, the treaty was debated in the U.S. Senate, which must ratify all foreign treaties by a two-thirds majority vote. Lawmakers worried that the "Pact of Paris," as the Kellogg-Briand Treaty was also known, would bind the United States to military action in distant locales, where the United States had no vital national interest. It might also prevent the country from defending itself against foreign invasion. Nevertheless, after the horrors of World War I, public opinion strongly favored the treaty.

The Senate generally supported the treaty but added important reservations: The United States had a right to **unilateral** action for self-defense and could not be forced to take action in case of treaty violations by other nations. In this form, the Kellogg-Briand Pact was supported by a vote of 85 to 1, with Republican John Blaine of Wisconsin casting the sole vote against it. The final version of the treaty was signed by 62 nations. Like the League of Nations, however, the Kellogg-Briand Pact did not succeed in ending war.

BREAKING THE TREATY

Two years after Japan signed the treaty, the Japanese army invaded Manchuria, a northern province of China. Neither the League of Nations nor the nations that had signed the Kellogg-Briand Pact took any action to prevent the Japanese occupation. In 1935, Italy, another member of the Kellogg-Briand Pact, invaded Ethiopia, a nation in eastern Africa.

Germany, another member of the pact, built up its military forces after the dictator Adolf Hitler (1933–1945) came to power in 1933. Claiming to act in defense of ethnic Germans in Czechoslovakia, Hitler ordered the invasion of the Sudetenland in 1938 and of the rest of Czechoslovakia in March 1939. Six months later, in September 1939, the German army invaded Poland, touching off World War II (1939–1945) in Europe. Without the means to enforce its provisions, the Kellogg-Briand Pact proved useless in preventing war, which could be defined as any aggressor nation saw fit.

IMPACT OF THE TREATY

Although it failed to prevent war, the Kellogg-Briand Pact did establish an internationally accepted doctrine: Self-defense is the only legal basis for war. (The pact is still in effect under U.S. federal law.) Following the example of the pact and the League of Nations, the United Nations has since passed provisions banning wars of aggression by its members.

See also: Treaty of Versailles; World War I; World War II.

Ku Klux Klan

Organization founded in Pulaski, Tennessee, shortly after the Civil War (1861–1865); it was first led by General Nathan Bedford Forrest of the defeated Confederacy, the group of states that seceded from the Union. The members of the early Klan fought against what they viewed as a hostile takeover of the South by Northern interests. After the **emancipation** of the slaves, Klan members also opposed—often with violence—the drive for rights and justice among the South's African Americans, seeing the freed slaves as a threat to Southern traditions and livelihoods. The Klan of the 1920s supported **isolationist** views and the retreat of the United States from foreign entanglements.

SPREAD OF THE KLAN

At the turn of the twentieth century, the Ku Klux Klan remained a small and strictly Southern organization. Then the group came under the control of professional publicity agents from Atlanta. **Anti-Semitism**, or hatred of the Jews, had reached a fever pitch in the city when Leo Frank, a Jewish factory owner, was accused of the rape and murder of a young worker named Mary Phagan. When his death sentence was commuted by the Georgia governor, Frank was kidnapped from his jail cell by a Klan group and **lynched**.

The horrible event brought national interest to the Klan and helped to inspire its rebirth. William Joseph Simmons took control of the national organization, proclaiming the founding of a new Klan at the summit of Stone Mountain, Georgia, in 1915. The D.W. Griffith film *Birth of a Nation,* a sympathetic portrayal of the Civil War–era Klan, inspired the use of white costumes and the practice of burning crosses. The Klan changed from a mostly Southern rural organization to a nationwide group with a strong presence in Northern cities.

THE NEW KLAN

The Klan was marketed to a national audience with a new wardrobe, a secret language and code, and an elaborate system of rank. Millions of new members joined the group and paid their annual "klecktokens" (dues). A "Great Migration" of African Americans from the South who were seeking new jobs in Northern cities such as Chicago, Detroit, and Cleveland also spurred Klan membership. In the "klaverns" (meeting places) organized in hundreds of cities, members shared their grievances against the many disruptive social changes of the 1920s, including the rapid growth of cities, **industrialization**, and changing norms of behavior.

In the 1920s, the organization grew particularly strong in the Midwest, where anti-immigrant and isolationist sentiment ran strong. The Klan promised to fight for "100 percent Americanism," meaning a ban on "undesirable" immigrants from southern and eastern Europe (a popular stand in the eastern United States) as well as Asia (popular out West). Strongly anti-Catholic as well, the Klan fought against private religious schools. In the state of Oregon, the Klan pushed legislators to pass a law requiring that all students attend public schools.

The Klan also drew on the fear among working-class Protestants that their jobs and livelihoods were under direct threat from **Socialists** and radical labor organizers. The Klan gathered thousands of members to local night meetings, paraded in full costume down the streets of Washington, D.C., and carried out lynchings of African Americans suspected of crimes or insults to the white population. Nationwide membership reached 6 million by 1924.

DECLINE OF THE KLAN

Bad publicity and scandal weakened the Klan of the 1920s. Although Klan members had reached political office in several states, the group faced rising opposition, hostile public hearings in the U.S. Congress, and public concern about the mayhem and disorder brought by Klan marches and lynchings. In Indiana, a Klan leader, Grand Dragon D.C. Stephenson, was convicted of rape and murder, an event that further ruined the national group's reputation.

Membership declined as the leaders of the Klan squabbled over money and territory. Politicians and newspapers denounced the Klan, while the traditional targets of the Klan formed their own associations to fight back. For example, the Anti-Defamation League (ADL) was organized to fight against the slandering of Jews. Although isolationist views and anti-immigrant sentiment remained strong, the Klan's antiwar stance further hurt the group after the United States entered World War II (1939–1945) in late 1941. By the end of the war, the organization was defunct, although it would rise in another form during the postwar **civil rights era**. The wide support of the Klan in the early part of the twentieth century demonstrates how deeply many Americans feared those who were perceived as different, as well as the nation's firm commitment to isolationism.

See also: Emergency Quota Act (1921); National Origins Act (1924); Red Scare.

FURTHER READING

MacLean, Nancy K. *Behind the Mask of Chivalry: The Making of the Second Ku Klux Klan.* New York: Oxford University Press, 1995.

Newton, Michael. *The Ku Klux Klan: History, Organization, Language, Influence, and Activities of America's Most Notorious Secret Society.* Jefferson, N.C.: McFarland and Company, 2006.

Wade, Wyn Craig. *The Fiery Cross: The Ku Klux Klan in America.* New York: Oxford University Press, 1998.

League of Nations

International organization created after World War I (1914–1918) to provide postwar stability and prevent future wars. A precursor to the United Nations, the league ultimately failed to achieve its objectives, due largely to the United States' **isolationist** stance and subsequent unwillingness to participate.

WILSON'S FOURTEEN POINTS

The League of Nations was the idea of President Woodrow Wilson (1913–1921) and a group of 150 scholars whom he commissioned. In January 1918, during costly and bloody World War I, Wilson spoke to Congress about a program for "peace without victory"—his Fourteen Points.

The most important of the Fourteen Points—and the most controversial in the U.S. Senate—was the creation of an international organization that would serve to protect its fellow members from foreign aggression.

THE LEAGUE AND THE TREATY OF VERSAILLES

Wilson went to the palace of Versailles, just outside Paris, in early 1919 to negotiate the terms of the war's end. Germany, heartened by the Fourteen Points, agreed to an **armistice** in November 1918. In the negotiations that followed, many of Wilson's Fourteen Points were left by the wayside. The president insisted, however, that the Treaty of Versailles include plans for the League of Nations.

Germany was especially hard-hit by the Treaty of Versailles. The nation lost its colonies and some of its territory and was forced to pay **reparations** to the Allies for war costs and damage. These harsh terms in part led to the national sentiment that brought the German dictator Adolf Hitler to power in 1933.

Wilson presented the Covenant of the League of Nations at the Versailles conference in February 1919. Among other things, the document provided for protection of nations' **sovereignty**, dispute resolution, and protection against foreign aggression. On June 28, 1919, 44 nations signed the covenant, creating the league. Now Wilson had to sell the concept to the American people—and, most importantly, secure **ratification** of the treaty by the U.S. Senate.

OPPOSITION

With peace in Europe achieved, Wilson returned to the United States in July 1919. He came home with the hope that Americans would support the Treaty of Versailles and the creation of the League of Nations. While he was abroad, however, sentiment had grown against the treaty and the league. In March 1919, 39 Republican senators and senators-elect, led by isolationists Henry Cabot Lodge and William E. Borah, prepared the "Round Robin Petition," which opposed the League of Nations.

Article X Lawmakers' discontent with the league and the treaty was focused on Article X of the covenant of the league, which stated:

> The members of the League undertake to respect and preserve against external aggression the territorial integrity and existing political independence of all Members of the League . . . .

Those who opposed the league believed that this clause left open the possibility that the United States could be dragged into a future conflict, and war-weary senators—and their constituents—did not want to see that happen.

Authority of the League vs. the UN

The League of Nations and the United Nations (UN) were established with similar aims: to peacefully settle international disputes; to prevent wars from breaking out and escalating; and to improve the lives of people all over the world. While the league was ineffective in achieving these aims, the United Nations has had more success.

The United Nations was established in 1945 with 51 original member states. The United Nations has had relative success in achieving its goal of "maintaining international peace and security." The starkest difference between it and the defunct League of Nations is its ability to mediate international disputes.

The league had far fewer active member nations—the United States had a seat at the league but never joined; Britain and France participated little; at its highest membership, it sat only 63 member countries. Thus, the league proved ineffective at preventing conflicts. Countries felt no safer because of the league's existence, and the goals of **disarmament** and peaceful interaction were not met.

The United Nations, by contrast, has been far more successful in its efforts to maintain peace. Volunteer troops, called peacekeepers, are present all over the world, helping to defuse armed conflicts like the Korean War (1950–1953) and aiding troops in the Iraqi War (2003-). The 15-member Security Council, while not bound to agree to resolutions, has made strides by condemning violence and **genocide**.

The United Nations has also received criticism for its handling of situations, namely, the genocide in Rwanda in 1994 and the ongoing genocide and conflict in Darfur, Sudan. On the whole, its successes in aiding and maintaining peace throughout the world have outweighed its failures—and the failures of the League of Nations.

TO THE PEOPLE

Because Wilson was determined to convince the American people that the League of Nations would be a benefit to the United States, he took his ideas directly to them. Beginning in Ohio in September 1919, he made 37 major speeches and traveled 8,000 miles (12,875 km) calling for the approval of the league. Public sentiment seemed to be turning in his favor.

Wilson's health began to deteriorate, however. He collapsed in September and soon after suffered a debilitating stroke that left him bedridden for months. With Wilson's campaign in support of the league at an end, there was nothing to prevent the Senate's rejection of the Treaty of Versailles. With the Senate's "nay" vote against the treaty and the league, the United States had isolated itself further from the international community.

MAKEUP OF THE LEAGUE

The League of Nations was divided into three parts. The Council, the league's main body, had five permanent members—France, Great Britain, Japan, Italy, and the United States, even though the United States never participated. The second part was the Assembly, representing all nations. The third part was a Secretariat, which supported the Council and the Assembly. The league first met in January 1920 in Geneva, Switzerland, a location chosen because of the **neutrality** of the Swiss.

LEAGUE SUCCESSES AND FAILURES
At its best, the League of Nations set many precedents for successful international law and diplomacy. The league established the Permanent Court of International Justice (PCIJ), or World Court, in 1920 at The Hague, Netherlands. The court served as judicial body for the world, wherein disputes between nations could be resolved. It handled international crises, allowing minority groups to air grievances, settling international diplomatic incidents, and resolving territorial disputes.

Diplomacy The league also represented a great step forward in international diplomacy. It made open discussion among nations—of trade, border disputes, and other conflicts—a common practice. It included all nations in the discussion, and it was the first international body with universal membership. The league made it routine to consider every problem as one common to the entire body. The hope was that in doing so peace between the nations would be cemented, as no nation would want to upset fellow league members.

Missteps However, the league's role in mediating violent conflicts between nations proved largely inefficient. It had little influence during the Spanish civil war (1936–1939) and took no action when Japan began invading China in the 1930s. Likewise, Italy's invasion of Ethiopia in 1935 brought no action, and Germany's steady incursion into parts of Europe was met with little but public condemnation. With the outbreak of World War II (1939–1945), the league's inability to stop acts of aggression was laid bare. From that point forward, it took little part in the world's affairs.

Dissolution of the League Its legitimacy dwindling, the League of Nations slowly stopped functioning as World War II unfolded. In late 1944, the league's holdings were transferred to the newly formed United Nations, and the final meeting of the league took place in April 1946.

See also: Borah, William E.; Fourteen Points; Lodge, Henry Cabot; Roosevelt, Franklin D.; World War I; World War II.

FURTHER READING
Rogers, James T. *Woodrow Wilson, Visionary for Peace. Makers of America.* New York: Facts On File, 1997.

Lend-Lease Act (1941)

Passed by Congress in March 1941, legislation authorizing economic and military aid to Great Britain as it fought in World War II (1939–1945). The Lend-Lease Act was a direct challenge to **isolationists** and signaled the end of U.S. neutrality in the growing European conflict.

AN ISOLATIONIST STANCE
After World War I (1914–1918) ended, the U.S. Senate rejected the Treaty of Versailles, which set the

terms of the peace between the warring nations and created the League of Nations. Politicians opposed U.S. membership in the league, insisting the United States should not be the "world's policeman."

Neutrality Acts After the bloodshed of World War I, the American people had grown tired of conflict. The U.S. Congress answered constituents with a shift toward a **nonintervention** policy. As a result, throughout the 1930s, Congress passed a series of laws known as the Neutrality Acts.

One of the laws made it illegal to lend money to any nation that had not repaid its debt from World War I. Another made it illegal for Americans to sell weapons to foreign countries. Still another ensured the United States would keep out of civil wars. All of the laws sent a strong signal: The United States would only deal with foreign countries in trade and business.

Growing Threat President Franklin D. Roosevelt (1933–1945) signed the Neutrality Acts into law, but did so begrudgingly. He believed that it was the responsibility of the United States to intervene to help preserve **democracy** and to turn back attempts to spread **tyranny**. He circumvented neutrality to send aid to China when Japan invaded in 1937, and he watched with growing worry the events unfolding in Europe.

WORLD WAR II UNFOLDS

By early 1941, World War II was fully under way. Japan had invaded China. Italy had invaded the African nation of Ethiopia, and German leader Adolf Hitler had invaded the European nations of Poland, Denmark, Norway, the Netherlands, Belgium, Luxembourg, and France. The only major nation in western Europe that had not been invaded by Nazi Germany was Great Britain.

In an attempt to force Great Britain into submission, Hitler's forces began bombing the island nation for months in late 1940. This bombardment and the air war between German and British warplanes over England were known as the Battle of Britain. President Roosevelt knew he had to help the U.S. ally withstand the Nazi assault, but first he needed to convince the American people that it was the right thing to do, while assuring them that aid did not mean direct U.S. participation in the war. In a speech in December 1940, he said:

> The people of Europe who are defending themselves do not ask us to do their fighting. They ask us for the implements of war, the planes, the tanks, the guns, the freighters, which will enable them to fight for their liberty and our security. Emphatically we must get these weapons to them in sufficient volume and quickly enough, so that we and our children will be saved the agony and suffering of war which others have had to endure . . .

With the support of U.S. citizens, Congress began crafting the Lend-Lease Act.

IMPLEMENTATION OF THE PROGRAM

Passed by Congress in March 1941, the Lend-Lease Act provided the president the power to "sell, transfer, exchange, lease, lend" ammunition, aircraft, ships, food, and other material essential to a war effort to any foreign government considered vital to the defense of the nation. The United States did not charge for those materials. It also allowed the use of American shipyards by those countries. At first, the act was aimed only at Great Britain. In April of the same year, the program was extended to China, and by late 1941, it had been extended to include the Soviet Union and other Allied powers.

Lend-Lease Program and the War
After the Japanese attack on Pearl Harbor on December 7, 1941, the United States joined the war. By then, however, thanks to Lend-Lease, U.S. industries were already well under way producing materials for the war effort. While the U.S. military took time to recruit and train soldiers for the war, the nation was already sending much-needed supplies to Allied forces overseas.

LEGACY
Lend-Lease expired in 1945, after the surrender of Japanese forces. By the end of the program, the United States had given or lent about $50 billion worth of materials to the Allied powers, a staggering amount for the time. That figure equals around $700 billion in 2009 prices. The program, and the eventual direct U.S. involvement in the war, helped to turn the tide against the Axis powers.

After the war, the United States never returned to its stance of isolationism. The nation invested money and troops in Western Europe to keep it free from possible **Communist**

takeovers and to avoid further wars. With the onset of the Cold War, the United States intervened in world affairs repeatedly in response to the Soviet Union's attempt to spread Communism, most notably with the Vietnam War (1965–1975).

See also: League of Nations; Pearl Harbor; Treaty of Versailles; World War I; World War II.

Lindbergh, Charles A. (1902–1974)

American aviator who made the first nonstop flight across the Atlantic Ocean in 1927 and became a national hero. Lindbergh later used his celebrity to promote an **isolationist** stance among the American people, reinforcing the idea that the United States should not become involved in foreign affairs.

EARLY LIFE
Charles Lindbergh was born on February 4, 1902, in Little Falls, Minnesota. His father, Charles Augustus Lindbergh, Sr., was a lawyer who in 1907 became a member of Congress. Young Charles was mechanically inclined. When he was 10, his mother took him to an air show, and it was clear that he had discovered his passion. In 1922, at age 20, Lindbergh moved to Nebraska. He attended a flight school, but it closed not long after he joined.

BECOMING A PILOT
Nevertheless, Lindbergh started his life as a stunt pilot. Although he did not yet have the skills to fly himself,

he joined a barnstorming group, a flying circus. There, Lindbergh performed wing walking and parachuting acts in order to earn money for more flying lessons. In 1923, Lindbergh got to fly on his own for the first time. He had bought himself a World War I (1914–1918) surplus "Jenny", and after only a half-hour lesson with another pilot, he decided to take to the air. Over the next week, he racked up five hours of flight time and then decided to make his first journey. He flew from Americus, Georgia, to Montgomery, Alabama. He spent the rest of 1923 and part of 1924 performing under the name "Aerial Daredevil Lindbergh."

Lindbergh prepares to board the *Spirit of St. Louis* at Roosevelt Field in New York and attempt the first solo transatlantic flight. The heroic feat not only made Lindbergh a national icon of bravery but also helped gather support for his antiwar campaign as events in Europe led to World War II.

MILITARY TRAINING

In 1924, Lindbergh joined the army. He wanted to become an Army Air Reserve pilot and reported for training in San Antonio, Texas, on March 19, 1924. Out of the 104 cadets who began training, only 18 graduated. Lindbergh was at the top of his class. He was made a 2nd Lieutenant in the Air Service Reserve Corps.

Soon after graduating, Lindbergh returned to barnstorming and giving flying lessons. In October 1925, his employer, the Robertson Aircraft Corporation, decided to establish an airmail route from St. Louis to Chicago. They wanted Lindbergh to plot the route's course and become their chief pilot. On April 15, 1926, Lindbergh was sworn in as an official mail carrier, trusted with the care and transportation of the U.S. mail.

NEW FEATS

During this time, Lindbergh learned of the Raymond Orteig Prize, a $25,000 prize for the first person to fly nonstop from New York to Paris. Lindbergh was determined to go for the prize. He convinced businessmen in St. Louis to back his venture and began building the *Spirit of St. Louis*. The plane was designed to maximize fuel capacity, sacrificing comfort and safety in the process. There was not even a parachute.

On May 20, 1927, at 7:52 A.M., Lindbergh took off from a dirt runway at Roosevelt Field on Long Island, New York. He landed in Le Bourget Field in France on May 21 at 10:21 P.M. local time. The flight took 33.5 hours. Lindbergh received numerous honors, including the Medal of Honor and the Distinguished Flying Cross. He was greeted back in the United States to a grand ticker-tape parade in New York City.

Following the flight, Lindbergh used his fame to promote the use of airmail. He never flew as a mail carrier again, but he would fly specific letters as public relations stunts. During one such flight, Lindbergh met Anne Morrow, the daughter of a respected U.S. diplomat, Dwight Morrow. In May 1929, they were married.

HORRIBLE CRIME

In March 1932, the Lindbergh family was at the center of one of the most celebrated crimes in American history. Lindbergh's infant son was kidnapped from his home and murdered. Many believe the child was accidentally killed as he was being taken. The kidnapper, however, dragged out the incident, demanding a **ransom**. A $50,000 ransom was paid, but the information the Lindberghs received in exchange was false. By chance, the child's body was discovered about two miles from the Lindberghs' home.

Move to Europe To escape the publicity after this terrible event, the Lindberghs moved to Europe.

Between 1935 and 1939, Lindbergh spent time overseas. This apparently gave him a different perspective on the events leading up to World War II (1939–1945). When he returned to the United States, he was very outspoken about keeping the United States out of the war. While the U.S. government wanted to intervene on behalf of Britain and France, Lindbergh told a different, more sympathetic story of the struggles in Germany. He believed that all the European nations were part of Western civilization and not destined for war or to destroy one another. Rather, he believed that all sides held some blame in the problems that led to World War II and that entering a war against Germany would not help to resolve those problems.

America First In September 1939, Lindbergh became the leading advocate for the America First Committee, an antiwar movement. Lindbergh believed that the destruction of Hitler's Germany would be devastating to Western civilization. It would leave a power vacuum in eastern Europe that would be filled by dictator Joseph Stalin's **Communist** Soviet Union, which in Lindbergh's view posed an even greater threat.

Lindbergh further claimed that the only groups pressuring the United States into war were the British, the Jews, and President Franklin D. Roosevelt's (1933–1945) administration. The Jews, he said, in particular should be careful about promoting war, as their existence depended on the tolerance of others, a quality often lost during times of war.

Many people, including his biographers, believe that Lindbergh was **anti-Semitic** and perhaps even a Nazi sympathizer. While he claimed not to hold anything against the Jews, he revealed his **prejudices** when he wrote in his diary that, "We must limit to a reasonable amount the Jewish influence.... Whenever the Jewish percentage of total population becomes too high, a reaction seems to invariably occur. It is too bad because a few Jews of the right type are, I believe, an asset to any country."

President Roosevelt was convinced that Lindbergh was a Nazi, and Nazi Germany often published his statements with fanfare. While Lindbergh was impressed with Hitler's reconstruction of Germany, he also expressed disgust when he later learned of the Nazi death camps and the **Holocaust**, in which more than 6 million Jews were murdered.

DURING THE WAR AND AFTER

While it is true that Lindbergh's isolationist stance helped Nazi Germany by keeping the United States out of the war, it is not clear that Lindbergh did it because he was a Nazi himself. Indeed, when the country finally did join World War II, Lindbergh asked to be reinstated in the military. President Roosevelt refused him, likely because of his earlier antiwar agitation. Denied entry to the military, Lindbergh began working with aviation companies to improve the design of warplanes. As a civilian technical representative, he flew combat missions in the Pacific and developed new techniques to use in the P-38, a bomber developed during the war.

The soldiers with whom he flew reported that he served with bravery.

Following World War II, Lindbergh retired to a life out of the public eye. President Dwight D. Eisenhower (1953–1961) restored his commission in the United States Air Force, and Lindbergh served as a consultant. He died on August 26, 1974, of cancer.

See also: America First Committee; Hitler, Adolf; World War II.

FURTHER READING

Berg, A. Scott. *Lindbergh*. New York: Berkley Trade, 1999.

Hixson, Walter L. *Charles A. Lindbergh: Lone Eagle*. Upper Saddle River, N.J.: Longman, 2006.

J–
L

Lodge, Henry Cabot (1850–1924)

American senator from Massachusetts most remembered for his opposition to the United States joining the League of Nations following World War I (1914–1918). Throughout his political career, Lodge was a dedicated **isolationist**. He played a central role in the rejection of the Treaty of Versailles by the U.S. Senate in 1920.

POLITICAL CAREER

In 1880, Lodge was elected to the state senate of Massachusetts. In 1886, he was elected to the U.S. House of Representatives, where he served for six years. Lodge was then elected to the U.S. Senate, where he had a major impact.

Lodge developed a friendly relationship with President Theodore Roosevelt (1901–1909) because of the president's support for a strong navy. Like Roosevelt, Lodge supported the Spanish-American War (1898) and the acquisition of the Philippines as a U.S. territory. However, Lodge was also a member of the conservative wing of the Republican Party, which led to disagreements with Roosevelt's **progressive** outlook and policies.

OPPOSITION TO WILSON

As a conservative, Lodge opposed the policies of Democratic president Woodrow Wilson (1913–1921). Specifically, Lodge supported high protective **tariffs** and wanted to keep the country on the gold standard, which required the government to keep a store of gold large enough to cover the redemption, if necessary, of all U.S. money in circulation.

Lodge was **interventionist** in his foreign policy views. Part of the attraction of acquiring the Philippines was to involve the United States more in world politics. As a major power with good moral foundations, he felt that the United States deserved to be a player on the international stage. When World War I broke out in Europe, Lodge strongly supported entering the war. However, he greatly disagreed with President Wilson's wartime policy. Wilson wanted to foster peace. Lodge felt that the president's idealism kept him from prosecuting the only kind of war that would be victorious: crushing Germany, both militarily and economically, so it could never again threaten the peace of Europe.

The conflict between Wilson and Lodge grew significantly after the 1918 congressional elections. Republicans gained control of the Senate in that election and Lodge became the majority leader (highest-ranking senator of the majority party), as well as head of the Foreign Relations Committee. This position allowed him to derail Wilson's plans for entering into the League of Nations following the close of the war.

LODGE AND THE LEAGUE

Lodge believed that the League of Nations would give foreign powers too much control over the United States. He did not want the country obliged to promises that it would not or could not keep. This did not mean, however, that he wanted the United States to withdraw from international affairs. Rather, he wanted the country to be free to decide what stances it would take, instead of deferring to another governing body. Specifically, he did not want the United States to be obligated to deploy troops in conflicts where the country had no important economic or political interests at stake.

To defeat the **ratification** of the Treaty of Versailles, which established the League of Nations, Lodge first deliberately delayed the voting. This gave him time to sway public opinion away from the treaty. By talking up the greatness of the national character, the U.S. system of government, and the country's place in history, Lodge was able to appeal to the people's sense of patriotism to turn them against joining the league. The United States, after all, had become an economic powerhouse without being involved in the political problems of Europe. It was a beacon of **democracy**.

In further attempts to defeat the treaty, Lodge continued to propose **amendments** to the treaty that he knew Wilson would not accept. The amendments would have weakened the league to the point of uselessness. Ultimately, the treaty was defeated, and the United States did not join the international peacekeeping body that it helped design. Ironically, despite his conviction that the United States should be involved in world affairs, Lodge's stance on the League of Nations has earned him the label of an isolationist.

In 1920, Lodge campaigned for Republican Warren G. Harding (1921–1923) for president. Harding later overturned many of Wilson's progressive laws. Lodge died on November 9, 1924. His personal account of the campaign against the League of Nations was published in the book *The Senate and the League of Nations*.

See also: Harding, Warren G.; League of Nations; Republican Party; Wilson, Woodrow; World War I.

M–N

Manchuria

See Japan.

Monroe Doctrine

First introduced in 1823, the Monroe Doctrine was a policy put forth by President James Monroe (1817–1825) warning European powers to avoid involvement in the dealings and affairs of countries in the Western Hemisphere. The policy amounted to a declaration of the **isolationist** stance of the United States that would endure throughout the nineteenth century.

BACKGROUND

By the early nineteenth century, the United States had grown significantly. The Louisiana Purchase in 1803 had doubled the nation's size, and Monroe's **annexation** of Florida from Spain in 1819 expanded the United States even farther. The idea of **manifest destiny**—a belief that the United States would eventually expand across North America—was flourishing.

Events near the United States and around the world, however, posed a threat to the young country. The nation had just successfully fought Great Britain in the War of 1812 (1812–1814). France and Spain had lost colonies in Latin America during the Napoleonic Wars but made clear their desire to reclaim them, leading to an uneasiness that these nations also would try to colonize parts of the North American continent. In addition, Russia's czar, Alexander II (1855–1881), had publicly expressed his interest in developing a **colony** on the Pacific Coast of North America.

History Speaks

Protecting the Hemisphere

On December 2, 1823, President James Monroe gave his State of the Union address to Congress. In his speech, he outlined a new policy toward Europe, in which **colonization** of nations in the Western Hemisphere would not be tolerated. His argument, which became known as the Monroe Doctrine, set the stage for an isolationist stance toward the world.

In the discussions to which this interest has given rise, and in the arrangements by which they may terminate the occasion has been judged proper for asserting, as a principle in which the rights and interests of the United States are involved, that the American continents, by the free and independent condition which they have assumed and maintain, are henceforth not to be considered as subjects for future colonization by any European powers. . . .

Of events in that quarter of the globe, with which we have so much intercourse, and from which we derive our origin, we have always been anxious and interested spectators. The citizens of the United States cherish sentiments the most friendly, in favor of the liberty and happiness of their fellow men on that side of the Atlantic. In the wars of the European powers, in matters relating to themselves, we have never taken any part, nor does it comport with our policy to do so. It is only when our rights are invaded, or seriously menaced, that we resent injuries, or make preparation for our defence. With the movements in this hemisphere, we are, of necessity, more immediately connected, and by causes which must be obvious to all enlightened and impartial observers.

We owe it, therefore, to candor, and to the amicable relations existing between the United States and those powers, to declare, that we should consider any attempt on their part to extend their system to any portion of this hemisphere, as dangerous to our peace and safety.

A SURPRISE OFFER

As these events unfolded, the United States received an offer of help where it least expected one. In October 1823, Great Britain suggested issuing a joint statement denouncing French and Spanish interference in Latin America. Its interest in the region was great: Having total dominance over shipping and trade in the world's oceans, Great Britain feared a threat to its control of the seas.

The offer was at first welcomed by American officials. President Monroe thought an alliance with Great Britain would send a message to the world that the United States was emerging as a global power. Secretary of State John Quincy Adams, however, was against the idea. He advised Monroe that joining with Great Britain in such a treaty would not signal power but weakness on the part of the United States.

THE POLICY

With Adams's opinion in mind, Monroe rejected Great Britain's offer and instead established a policy for the United States only. In December 1823, Monroe outlined the policy, written by Adams, in his State of the Union address. First, he said, the United States would allow no further colonies to be set up in the Western Hemisphere. Second, he warned against any involvement by European nations in Latin America. Third, he said that the United States would not play a role in dealings between existing Latin American colonies and their European rulers.

Though unenforceable and more a statement of purpose than actual policy, the Monroe Doctrine, as it came to be known, established the United States as the "overseer" of the Western Hemisphere. More importantly, it isolated the United States, and the hemisphere, from the rest of the world and set the tone of noninterference for decades to come.

FURTHER READING

Joy, Mark S. *American Expansionism, 1783–1860*. London: Pearson Education, 2003.

Samuels, Richard J., ed. *Encyclopedia of United States National Security*. Thousand Oaks, Calif.: Sage Publications, 2006.

Mussolini, Benito (1883–1945)

Italian dictator credited with helping develop the political doctrine of **Fascism.** Mussolini joined forces with German dictator Adolf Hitler (1933–1945) before the outbreak of World War II (1939–1945), making Italy one of the Axis powers along with Japan. Later, in 1941, after the Japanese attacked the American naval base in Pearl Harbor, Hawaii, the United States was drawn into the war, thus ending the nation's **isolationist** foreign policy.

EARLY LIFE

Benito Mussolini was born on July 29, 1883, in Predappio, Italy. His father, Alessandro Mussolini, was a blacksmith, journalist, and Socialist. His mother, Rosa Maltoni, was a teacher. Mussolini's family was poor, a fact that he used later in his political career to promote himself as one of the common people.

Mussolini was a poor student. He was sent to a boarding school run by Salesian monks, in deference to his mother's religious beliefs, but he rebelled against their teaching and strict discipline. He became violent, stabbing one student with a knife and attacking a monk who tried to discipline him. Mussolini was expelled from the school after a second attack on a student.

M–N

Adolf Hitler at his side, Italian dictator Benito Mussolini salutes a crowd at a rally in Munich, Germany, in 1937. The territorial ambition of these Fascist dictators touched off World War II and eventually served to end the isolationist foreign policy of the United States.

In 1902, Mussolini moved north to Switzerland to avoid his mandatory military service in Italy. He was 19 years old and had no money. He worked odd jobs, living from day to day. He also developed a diverse political philosophy. Based on his ideas, he was able to speak to fellow **Socialists** in Switzerland with persuasion and confidence.

In 1904, Mussolini was arrested in Switzerland for vagrancy and returned to Italy. He was forced to fulfill his military service. Once he was discharged, however, he threw himself into politics. Mussolini was gaining a reputation as a powerful speaker for the Socialist cause.

RISE TO POWER

In 1912, Mussolini earned a position of power in the Socialist Party Congress and took over editing their newspaper, *Avanti!* Mussolini's editorials stirred young Socialists to action and he doubled the newspaper's circulation. At first, Mussolini vehemently opposed Italy joining World War I (1914–1918), but he came to believe in the socioeconomic thinker Karl Marx's statement that participation in war was often the necessary precursor to revolution.

To bring his ideas of revolution to Italy, Mussolini needed the country to enter the conflict. His editorials began to support entering the war on the side of France as strongly as he had previously opposed it. For his reversal, he was thrown out of the Socialist Party; he then left his position at *Avanti!*

Mussolini left Italy to join the Italian forces fighting in World War I. When he returned, however, he was a staunch anti-Socialist, totally opposing the viewpoints he had held before the war. In 1918, he had already begun calling for a strong dictator to remake Italy, politically and economically. In 1919, he formed a political party in the city of Milan with the intent of making himself such a dictator. He called his group of supporters *fasci di combattimento,* or "fighting bands." They were made up of revolutionaries, disenchanted Socialists,

anarchists, and ex-soldiers. Fascism was born.

Mussolini's speeches to the people were above all dramatic. Though his facts were often wrong and his ideas contradictory, he spoke with a power, eloquence, and vigor to which many Italians were drawn. His rallies were like theater. Through this personal charisma, his influence grew. Italians began forming themselves in Fascist militia groups. They hunted down Socialists, terrorized towns, and burned union headquarters. Mussolini did not have to organize these squads personally, as they worked on their own with his encouragement. They disrupted Italy's left-wing government and prevented it from exerting control and ensuring law and order.

In 1921, Mussolini won a seat in the Italian Parliament along with 35 other Fascists. That same year, the National Fascist Party was formed, with Mussolini as its leader. In 1922, Mussolini led the National Fascist Party in the March on Rome. The trade unions had called for a general strike, and Mussolini stated that if the government did not stop the strike, then he and his Fascist Party would. The government did nothing. In turn, the prime minister was ousted, and the Italian king offered Mussolini control of the government.

MUSSOLINI'S GOVERNMENT

While Mussolini's first government was a **coalition,** made up of Fascists, nationalists, and liberals, his goal was clear: a **totalitarian state** under his rule. Under Italian law, the legislature could give the prime minister dictatorial powers for one year. Mussolini forced the legislature to grant him this authority. His goal was unlimited power for himself and the transformation of Italy into a Fascist dictatorship.

Mussolini integrated the Fascist militias, known as the Blackshirts, with the Italian military. Notably, he forced the legislature to pass the Acerbo Law, which give Fascists control of the government. While Mussolini was in power, his party did not have a majority of Parliament seats. The law stated that whichever party had the largest share of votes, providing it was more than 25 percent, would be given two-thirds of the seats in Parliament. This meant that Mussolini did not have to worry about losing his position of power.

FASCISTS IN CONTROL

By and large, most Italians welcomed Mussolini's seizing of power. They wanted a stable government and a sound economy. If Mussolini's dictatorship could bring them those things, then they were generally willing to submit. Whether they knew what the cost would be is unclear.

Soon, the Fascists outlawed trade unions, all other political parties, and the free press. Free speech was eliminated. The Italian people were put under the eye of secret police. The kidnap and murder of political opponents became a hallmark of Mussolini's rule.

Despite attempts at reform and public works, life for a working-class Italian continued to be difficult. The average Italian worker earned a fraction of what workers in Britain and

M–N

France earned. Mussolini offered no policy to help them. Instead, business tycoons who had supported his regime were helped by new trade policies and began to turn a profit.

FASCIST FOREIGN POLICY

Mussolini made his most damaging mistakes in the field of foreign policy. Driven by national pride, he sought to return Italy to its ancient glory during the times of the Roman Empire. He sought power by taking colonies in Africa and expanding Italy's borders in Europe. This led to war with Ethiopia in 1935 and 1936. While the war was internationally condemned, no nation did anything to stop it. Mussolini took over Ethiopia, establishing the basis of the Italian empire of which he had dreamed.

In April 1939, Italy invaded the small Balkan nation of Albania. Italy defeated Albania in just five days, forcing the Albanian king to flee. Mussolini made Albania a part of Italy's growing empire. Mussolini also had imperial designs on Tunisia and other parts of North Africa, but he did not succeed in taking over these lands until 1942.

Until May 1939, the alliance between Italy and Germany had not been official. In that month, however, the Pact of Steel treaty was signed, outlining the "friendship and alliance" between the two nations. After the Nazi invasion of Poland on September 1, 1939, which sparked World War II, Italy remained neutral in the war. Not until June 1940 did Italy join Germany by declaring war on Great Britain and France.

Throughout the war, most of Mussolini's military actions were disastrous. The Germans had to save the Italian army from certain defeat several times. It soon became clear from the numerous defeats that Italy was likely to lose its war against the **Allies**. On July 24, 1943, Mussolini's own party voted to oust him from the government. The Italian king had him arrested and Mussolini was imprisoned in a remote region of mountainous northern Italy. Nevertheless, the German army managed to rescue him and bring him to Munich.

From Munich, Mussolini tried to set up a rival Fascist government in northern Italy, but it was unsuccessful. The Fascists who still controlled Italy remained allied with Hitler and were continuing the fight without Mussolini's help. As the Allies advanced on Italy, the Italian government decided to execute Mussolini. Before they could, however, he attempted to escape to the mountains. On April 28, 1945, Mussolini and his mistress, Clara Petacci, were recognized during their escape and killed. Their bodies were hung in Milan, to the joy of the Italian people.

See also: Axis Powers; Hitler, Adolf; World War I; World War II.

FURTHER READING

Bosworth, R.J.B. *Mussolini's Italy: Life Under the Fascist Dictatorship, 1915–1945.* New York: Penguin Books, 2007.

Hibbert, Christopher. *Mussolini: The Rise and Fall of Il Duce.* New York: Palgrave Macmillan, 2008.

National Origins Act (1924)

Law passed as part of the Immigration Act of 1924, which further restricted the number of **immigrants** to the United States from any single country. The passage of this law was, in part, a result of the **isolationist** sentiments of U.S. lawmakers and voters at this time.

Before the bill was passed, anti-immigrant feelings had been running high in the United States for many years. This was because of a dramatic change in the ethnic makeup of new arrivals. Since the beginning of the twentieth century, southern Europeans had been moving into New York and other eastern U.S. cities. From Italy, Greece, and the Slavic countries of eastern Europe, foreigners crowded into unhealthy city **ghettos,** worsening the public's fears of rising crime, contagious disease, and dangerous political movements, including **communism** and **anarchy**.

UNFOUNDED FEARS

Writers such as Madison Grant and Lothrop Stoddard proclaimed the country's original ethnic makeup—mostly English, German, Dutch, and Scandinavian Protestants—to be under a dire threat. In his book *The Rising Tide of Color against White World Supremacy,* Stoddard expressed a common belief that "We will never . . . be the race we might have been if America had been reserved for the descendants of the picked Nordics of colonial times." In the minds of many leaders, the United States remained an offshoot of England and northern Europe. Its culture, religion, democratic politics and **republican** government were a product of northern European thought. The very different traditions brought by people of other nations, in this view, would radically change the country's outlook and end the liberties guaranteed by the Declaration of Independence and the Constitution.

An influx of Asians on the West Coast and Mexicans from south of the border also posed an economic threat. It was widely believed that increased competition for scarce jobs would drive down wages and impoverish ordinary workers. A series of laws already had excluded Chinese workers, who were no longer needed for the task of building railroads across the western mountains.

LEGISLATING IMMIGRATION

To deal with the "threat," Congress passed the Immigration Act of 1924, also known as the Johnson-Reed Act, named for cosponsors Albert Johnson and David Reed. The law limited the total number of immigrants to 165,000. The number of immigrants from any single country was limited to 2 percent of the number of people from that country living in the United States in 1890, as measured by the national **census** of that year. People from Asia were excluded entirely (since 1790, they had been ineligible for citizenship). North American immigrants were free of any **quota** whatsoever.

The law established the system of immigration visas, issued by American consulates in foreign countries, which is still in use. It was later replaced by the Immigration and Nationality Act of 1952.

See also: Emergency Quota Act (1921).

FURTHER READING

Dinnerstein, Leonard. *Ethnic Americans: A History of Immigration.* New York: Columbia University Press, 1999.

Graham, Otis. *Unguarded Gates: A History of America's Immigration Crisis.* Lanham, Md.: Rowman & Littlefield, 2006.

Swain, Carol M., ed. *Debating Immigration.* New York: Cambridge University Press, 2007.

National Socialist (Nazi) Party

See Hitler, Adolf.

Neutrality Acts

See Lend-Lease Act (1941); Republican Party.

Nye, Gerald P. (1892–1971)

United States senator and leader in the Republican Party opposed to the United States joining World War II (1939–1945). Nye hoped that the nation would retain its **isolationist** foreign policy.

EARLY CAREER

In 1916, Nye married Anna Margaret Munch, and together they moved to Fryburg, North Dakota. Nye bought Fryburg's newspaper, the *Weekly Pioneer*, and worked as its editor for three years. The couple moved again in 1919, this time to Cooperstown, Griggs County, North Dakota. Nye became editor of the *Sentinel Courier*. Notably, in his editorials for the paper, he promised to fight for the local farmers. He advised them to join together to fight the forces of big business, a crusade he would carry with him into politics.

ENTRY INTO POLITICS

Nye's introduction to politics shocked everyone, no one more than himself. On June 25, 1925, North Dakota's senator, Edwin F. Ladd, died. It was the duty of North Dakota's governor to select a replacement, so he called in newspapermen from around the state to hear the news. All were eager to find out who would be replacing the late senator. The governor then announced that he had chosen Gerald Nye. Nye was stunned.

He took the appointment, however, and moved to Washington, D.C. Despite lacking the polish of a Washington politician, Nye brought youthful enthusiasm to the office. The people of North Dakota approved and returned him to office in the 1926 congressional election. He was appointed to a number of committees, including the Appropriations Committee and Defense Committee. As a Progressive, Nye generally supported President Franklin D. Roosevelt's (1933–1945) **New Deal** policies, although he felt that they did not go far enough to address the country's economic problems. He also felt that Roosevelt was too concerned with big business and not concerned enough with small farmers.

NYE'S LEGACY

Nye's biggest impact was made through the Nye Committee, also called the Special Committee on Investigation of the Munitions Industry. In spring 1934, Dorothy Detzer, head of Women's International League for Peace and Freedom, along with Senator George Norris of Nebraska, convinced Nye to begin investigating the munitions industry for its part in pushing the United States into World War I (1914–1918). As the Senate seemed largely unconcerned with the issue, it allowed the committee to form and begin hearings. The committee found that American weapons manufacturers routinely bribed foreign officials to increase sales. The committee further concluded that some American companies were war profiteers and "merchants of death" and recommended to President Roosevelt that heavy taxes be imposed to limit the profits of war. To Nye's great surprise, the president agreed.

Nye also pushed for a **neutrality** bill in Congress. He wanted to outlaw the selling of arms to any country at war. Americans were generally in favor of neutrality at the time. People did not want to get involved in yet another European disaster. As part of his antiwar activism, Nye also gave his support to the American First Committee, whose most famous spokesman was pilot Charles A. Lindbergh.

Despite his efforts to keep the United States out of World War II (1939–1945), Nye voted along with the rest of the Senate in declaring war on Japan, following the bombing of Pearl Harbor, Hawaii. In 1944, Nye lost reelection to the Senate. He chose to stay in the Washington area, setting up a recordkeeping business. On July 17, 1971, Nye died from an allergic reaction to a drug he had been wrongly prescribed. Despite Nye's support of isolationism, he was unable to prevent the United States from entering World War II.

See also: America First Committee; Japan; Lindbergh, Charles A.; Pearl Harbor; World War I; World War II.

M–N

P–R

Palmer Raids

A series of arrests carried out at the height of the Red Scare, a fear of a Communist takeover of the U.S. government. The fear of Communism and other alien political doctrines strengthened during World War I (1914–1918) grew in the postwar years and continued through the early 1920s. Under the direction of the Department of Justice and Attorney General A. Mitchell Palmer, local police and federal agents took thousands of **anarchists, Socialists,** and **immigrants** into custody, in many cases without arrest warrants, and charged them with conspiring to overthrow the government and other crimes. The public's support of the Palmer raids drew on the widespread **isolationist** sentiment in the aftermath of World War I. By the early 1920s, however, opposition from members of Congress, criticism in the press, and public ridicule of Palmer himself eventually brought the Palmer raids and the Red Scare to an end.

GROWING FEARS

The fear of **anarchy** intensified during World War I. President Woodrow Wilson (1913–1921) and other American leaders had warned of sabotage, or subversive attempts at disruption, and other hostile acts carried out by foreign agents.

The 1917 Russian Revolution raised the suspicion that a **Bolshevik** revolution might be afoot in the United States. The Bolsheviks, a radical wing of the Russian Socialist Party, had seized power in the Russian capital of St. Petersburg, murdered the Russian czar and his family, and signed a separate peace agreement with Germany. Their leader, Vladimir I. Lenin, promised a future world revolution of industrial workers—a promise taken seriously by business leaders and politicians in Europe and the United States. Congress responded to the threat with the 1918 Sedition Act, which made a federal crime of advocating the overthrow of the government, as well as any public expression against the war.

The defeat of Germany by the Allied powers in 1918 was followed by riot and rebellion in many German cities. This turmoil inspired Socialists in Europe and the United States to predict the imminent overthrow of the **capitalist** system, which they held responsible for starting the war. In 1919, two new Communist political parties formed in the United States: the Communist Party and the Communist Labor Party. That year, several bombings took place in American cities for which anarchist groups claimed credit.

SILENCING OPPOSITION

The Bureau of Investigation, a branch of the U.S. Department of Justice, had been following anarchist suspects for several years. In 1919, under Palmer's direction, the bureau formed the General Intelligence Division under the direction of J. Edgar Hoover. According to the Espionage Act of 1917, publishing newspapers or pamphlets that criticized the actions of the U.S. government could be punished with up to 20 years in prison. Under the terms of the Sedition Act of 1918, the department had been authorized to identify all persons advocating violence against the government; the Department of Labor was responsible for deporting suspects. An Anarchist Exclusion Act also authorized the United States to bar "aliens who believe in or advocate the overthrow by force or violence of the Government of the United States." Hoover gathered a list of more than 150,000 suspicious persons and organized an immense card file, which he used to record the actions of suspected anarchists, Socialists, and other opponents of the American government.

On June 2, 1919, a series of bombings hit Washington, D.C.; New York; and Boston. One of the targets was the Washington home of A. Mitchell Palmer, where a bomb exploded in the hands of an anarchist approaching the front door. The bomber was blown to pieces; fragments of an anarchist pamphlet fluttered to the street and into Palmer's front yard.

The incident deeply frightened the attorney general, who now saw the radicals as a personal threat and the fight against Socialism as a springboard to a run for the presidency. President Wilson, who was preoccupied with passage of the Treaty of Versailles by Congress, gave Palmer his unspoken support, while the press and public called for action.

DEPORTING RADICALS

Relying on Hoover's files and the federal anti-sedition laws, bureau agents swung into action in major cities throughout the country in November 1919. Carrying blank warrants, the agents rounded up labor activists, Communist Party members, suspected anarchists, and innocent bystanders. The agents seized records, books, letters, and subscription lists for radical journals such as *Mother Earth*. Shortly afterward, a group of 249 suspected radical leaders, including Emma Goldman, founder of *Mother Earth*, were taken to Ellis Island and then shipped out on the U. S.S. *Buford* for permanent relocation to Russia.

Palmer justified the raids with a series of newspaper articles in which he warned of a looming revolution. In January 1920, in an even larger series of raids on private homes, hotels, and offices, officials rounded up more than 4,000 suspects in 30 cities. Trials of the suspects began in the spring. By this time, however, the Palmer raids were raising opposition among several senators and from Louis Post, secretary of the Department of Labor, who saw to it that the accused were allowed lawyers and a fair hearing. When Post accused Palmer of overstepping his bounds, Palmer responded with the prediction of a Socialist revolution to take place on May Day, 1920. May 1 came and went with no violence, however. Discredited and ridiculed in the press, Palmer quickly disappeared from the spotlight, and the Palmer raids came to an end. Despite the end of the raids, however, isolationist feelings continued to grow in the United States throughout the 1920s and 1930s.

See also: Ku Klux Klan; Emergency Quota Act (1921); Red Scare; World War I.

FURTHER READING

Finan, Chris. *From the Palmer Raids to the Patriot Act: A History of the Fight for Free Speech in America*. Boston: Beacon Press, 2008.

Murray, Robert K. *Red Scare: A Study in National Hysteria*. Minneapolis: University of Minnesota Press, 2009.

P– R

Pearl Harbor

American military base on the island of Oahu, Hawaii, and the site of the surprise attack by the Japanese navy and air force on U.S. military facilities on December 7, 1941. The Japanese attack on Pearl Harbor brought an abrupt end to the isolationism that had prevented the Roosevelt administration (1933–1945) from taking part in World War II (1939–1945). The attack dealt heavy damage to the U.S. military, prompting the nation to a declaration of war and a full-scale effort against the Axis powers.

JAPANESE AGGRESSION

Since the end of World War I (1914–1918) in 1918, Japan had been

The USS *California* burns during the Japanese attack on Pearl Harbor, on December 7, 1941. The surprise attack, and an inspiring speech by President Franklin D. Roosevelt, led to a declaration of war by the U.S. Congress the next day.

Russia after the Russian Revolution, Japan now found itself confronting the United States for control of resources and territory in Asia and the western Pacific.

Political and Economic Concerns Politics within Japan played an important role in these events. During the 1920s, the Japanese government came under the control of a strongly **nationalistic** class of military officers who had great influence over the Japanese emperor. These officers saw democratic, representative government as working against the country's interests. When the **Great Depression** of the 1930s brought unemployment and poverty, the Japanese government saw the control of resources in Asia as the country's sole means of escaping from an economic disaster.

Invasion of Manchuria Japan attacked and occupied Manchuria, a northern province of China, in 1931. In the following years, the Japanese army extended its occupation to most of eastern China. The United States and the League of Nations protested atrocities committed by the Japanese military in Chinese cities, but to no effect. Japan withdrew from the League of Nations and signed an alliance with Nazi Germany and Italy, joining the Axis powers.

ECONOMIC AND DIPLOMATIC BATTLES
On September 1, 1939, the invasion of Poland by Nazi Germany touched off World War II in Europe. While Britain and France declared war on Germany, the United States stayed

aggressively expanding its economic and political control of East Asia. Having reached the limits of its expansion in North America, the United States was projecting its naval power further into the Pacific Ocean from the east. After its victory in the Spanish-American War in 1898, the United States had colonized the Philippines, a group of islands lying due south of Japan in southeastern Asia. Having fought alongside the United States during World War I, and cooperated with American action in eastern

Then & Now

Pearl Harbor and 9/11

Like the Pearl Harbor attack, the terrorist attacks of September 11, 2001, delivered a frightening shock to a nation seeking to avoid the bloodshed and complications of a distant conflict. At Pearl Harbor, the Japanese military delivered a well-planned and closely coordinated blow to the American military, killing more than 2,000 people and destroying a dozen naval ships and nearly 200 aircraft. The intent of the Japanese was to cripple the military ability of the United States. The effort failed as the nation regrouped, drove its armed forces across the Pacific Ocean, and destroyed Japanese cities and industry from the air.

While the attack on Pearl Harbor was carried out by an organized national military, the attacks of September 11, 2001, were coordinated by a small and secretive international terrorist group, al Qaeda ("The Base" in Arabic), which had civilians hijack planes and then use them as flying missiles, targeted at civilians and key buildings. The World Trade Center, the Pentagon, and a third target (possibly the U.S. Capitol or the White House) were symbolic rather than military targets, which represented the economic, political, and military might of the United States. Al Qaeda's intent was twofold: to damage the American economy and to incite a counterattack that would bring the United States into conflict with Islamic nations in the Middle East. The United States responded with invasions of Afghanistan and Iraq and vowed to carry on a fight against terrorism around the world.

This particular conflict, however, is not likely to have a clear-cut ending, as did World War II. Al Qaeda is inspired by religious doctrine; rather than control of territory or resources, it seeks to establish Islamic states ruled on the strict principles of Islamic law. Rather than a military conflict, the war on terrorism declared by the United States in the wake of 9/11 is more of an ideological battle—one that will continue as long as two very different philosophies strive for global dominance.

out of the war, extending only economic aid and the lease of war material to its allies.

In 1940, in retaliation for the continued occupation of China by Japan, the U.S. government **embargoed**, or stopped, all shipments of airplanes, spare parts, and aviation fuel to Japan, although exports of crude oil continued. The Japanese government considered this **sanction** an act of provocation.

U.S. Aid Since the start of the war in 1939, the Roosevelt administration had won support for increasing military spending. In June 1940, Roosevelt signed the Naval Expansion Act, which funded the construction of new battleships, aircraft carriers, and military airplanes. The president won **bipartisan** support for this effort, even though Republicans in Congress had long opposed the government's spending on New Deal programs to combat the Great Depression. War manufacturing created an important incentive for the American economy and full employment for U.S. workers. Building weapons, tanks, and military aircraft would double the nation's **gross national product (GNP)** by the end of the war.

Military and Diplomatic Actions The Japanese military began planning a surprise attack that would prevent any challenge by the United States to Japanese control of the Pacific. Rather than the U.S. mainland, however, the Japanese targeted Pearl Harbor, a military base in the U.S. territory of Hawaii. The plan was to damage American naval power and airpower, and in particular American aircraft carriers. These ships were the most effective means of projecting airpower into the far reaches of the Pacific region.

In the meantime, the Roosevelt administration pursued diplomatic means of keeping the peace with Japan. High-level contacts between the two countries, however, grew increasingly hostile. Having cracked Japanese codes, U.S. intelligence agencies were studying Japanese diplomatic and military communications. By December 1941, it became obvious to senior military officers that Japan was planning a major assault, although the precise location and time were not clear. It was widely believed among both military and civilian leaders that Japan would strike at British possessions, and possibly the Philippines, before daring a direct attack on U.S. territory. Although President Franklin D. Roosevelt considered a first strike to head off the Japanese, he rejected the idea on the grounds that the United States should not be seen as the aggressor nation in the coming conflict.

A DATE WHICH WILL LIVE IN INFAMY

The attack on Pearl Harbor began in the dawn hours of December 7, 1941. Six Japanese aircraft carriers launched 353 fighters and torpedo bombers, while a small fleet of midget submarines entered Pearl Harbor to launch torpedoes. The attack resulted in 2,402 civilian and military deaths, the sinking of four major battleships and a dozen other naval ships, and the loss of 188 military aircraft.

The Japanese achieved complete surprise, although the aircraft carriers that were the most important target of the attack were at sea and escaped any harm. In addition, the Japanese neglected to target the U.S. submarine fleet (which would prove to be a decisive weapon in the Pacific war), as well as crucial fuel installations and ship maintenance and intelligence facilities. With Pearl Harbor still intact, the United States was soon able to begin action against the Japanese navy in the Pacific.

War! Isolationists in Congress and among the public immediately lost support. The initial shock of the attack turned into a nearly unanimous desire for revenge. On the day after the attack, President Roosevelt delivered a stirring radio address to a joint session of the U.S. Congress, declaring that:

> Yesterday, December 7th, 1941—a date which will live in infamy—the United States of America was suddenly and deliberately attacked by naval and air forces of the Empire of Japan . . . .

I believe that I interpret the will of the Congress and of the people when I assert that we will not only defend ourselves to the uttermost, but will make it very certain that this form of treachery shall never again endanger us.

Hostilities exist. There is no blinking at the fact that our people, our territory, and our interests are in grave danger.

With confidence in our armed forces, with the unbounding determination of our people, we will gain the inevitable triumph— so help us God.

I ask that the Congress declare that since the unprovoked and dastardly attack by Japan on Sunday, December 7th, 1941, a state of war has existed between the United States and the Japanese empire.

Congress immediately passed a declaration of war against Japan, which Roosevelt signed on the same day. A declaration of war by Nazi Germany on the United States brought the United States into the European theater as well.

End of Isolationism The attack on Pearl Harbor promptly ended calls from isolationists in the United States to stay out of the war. The executive board of the America First Committee voted unanimously to dissolve the organization, and its leaders announced their public support of the war effort. Charles A. Lindbergh, a leading figure of the America First Committee, requested a reinstatement of his military commission— which President Roosevelt refused.

Lindbergh, thought by some to be a Nazi sympathizer, eventually took part as an air observer in the Pacific theater and flew more than 20 combat missions against the Japanese.

Over the next few months, the U.S. military regrouped. The first major battle of the Pacific theater took place among the Midway Islands, lying northwest of Hawaii. U.S. planes and carriers scored a major victory in this battle, all but crippling an entire Japanese force and sinking four enemy aircraft carriers.

Blame for The Attack At the same time, accusations were echoing in Congress over the failure of the government and the military to prepare for the attack at Pearl Harbor. Secretary of the Navy Frank Knox ordered an immediate investigation. Admiral Husband Kimmel, overall commander of the navy in the Pacific theater, and Major General Walter Short, the army's commander in Hawaii, were relieved of their duties 10 days after the attack.

These measures did not satisfy Republican opponents of the Roosevelt administration, many of whom remained strongly isolationist in outlook. Roosevelt was accused of knowing an attack was planned and imminent, and of doing nothing to prevent it. His motive, according to this theory, was to allow the Japanese attack to go forward in order to provide a clear-cut justification for entering the war against the Axis powers. Roosevelt's isolationist critics also believed that the economic **boycott** by the United States of Japan and hostile diplomacy on the part of the United

States represented a deliberate provocation that the Japanese were bound to answer with military action.

The Roberts Commission To answer the public outcry over Pearl Harbor, Roosevelt asked Owen Roberts, a Supreme Court justice, to convene a commission to investigate the attack and military readiness at Pearl Harbor. The Roberts Commission concluded that an intelligence breakdown had occurred at the highest levels of the military. In addition, the military was derelict in not preparing to meet an attack on Hawaii, even though Kimmel and Short had been warned in January 1941 by Secretary Knox that such an attack was a likely method for Japan to start a war with the United States.

The Roberts Commission also found that on the morning of December 7 the army's early warning radar system on Hawaii was not working; that antiaircraft guns were not manned and ready; and that fighter aircraft on the ground were not in position to quickly scramble and meet an attack (the planes had been positioned this way to discourage sabotage on the ground, which General Short feared more than a surprise attack from the air). In addition, the traditional rivalry between the armed services had played a role, as Kimmel and Short had not coordinated their defensive preparations.

THE END OF ISOLATIONISM
Many historians mark Pearl Harbor as a crucial turning point in the history of American isolationism. Although the United States had, since the time of George Washington, made an effort to avoid "foreign entanglements," the rise of American military and economic power brought the country into closer contact with the rest of the world. The presence of oceans to the east and west, and peaceful countries to the north and south, did not allow the United States to ignore events in Europe and Asia. By the 1920s, the occupation of Hawaii, the Philippines, and other territories in the Pacific region was bringing the United States into direct conflict with the expanding Japanese empire. In Europe, the U.S. government had allied with Britain and France and against Hitler's Germany.

U.S. POLICY AFTER THE WAR
In the years following World War II, the United States helped to rebuild Europe. The country offered economic aid in the form of the Marshall Plan, which tied the United States closely to the nations of Western Europe and helped to prevent the spread of **communism** from Soviet-allied states in central and Eastern Europe. U.S. military units were stationed in Japan and former Japanese colonies in the Pacific, ensuring both military and economic cooperation from the new Japanese government. Isolationism (or **noninterventionism** in the words of its supporters) became the stance of only a minority as the United States fought anti-Communist wars in Korea (1950–1953) and Vietnam (1959–1975).

See also: America First Committee; Axis Powers; Japan; World War II.

FURTHER READING

Hoyt, Edwin Palmer. *Pearl Harbor.* Boston: G.K. Hall, 2000.

Kimmett, Larry, and Margaret Regis. *The Attack on Pearl Harbor: An Illustrated History.* Navigator Publishers, 1999.

Lord, Walter. *Day of Infamy.* New York: Henry Holt, 2001.

Prange, Gordon. *At Dawn We Slept: The Untold Story of Pearl Harbor.* New York: Penguin Books, 1982.

Red Scare

A fear of revolution that swept across the United States during and immediately after the end of World War I (1914–1918). The Red Scare increased **isolationist** feelings among the American people.

ROOTS IN RUSSIA

An uprising against the Russian government brought the radical **Bolshevik** wing of the Russian **Socialist** Party to power in late 1917. Under the leadership of Vladimir I. Lenin, the Bolsheviks began a systematic effort to impose a **Communist** economic system on their nation, after the ideas of the German historian and economist Karl Marx.

As a result, private property was confiscated, all industries came under government control, and power was centralized in the hands of Bolshevik-led committees, or soviets, which were appointed by party leaders. The Bolsheviks withdrew Russia from the war against Germany and signed a separate peace agreement. They also threatened to spread revolution to western Europe and the rest of the **capitalist** world.

U.S. Reaction In the United States, the Socialist revolution in Russia was seen as a very serious danger. After the United States joined the **Allies** in April 1917, Congress passed a series of laws intended to thwart any opposition to the government and the war. The Espionage and Sedition Acts set down harsh punishments for any public criticism of the government's war effort; among the many people prosecuted under these laws was the Socialist labor leader Eugene V. Debs.

The **armistice** of November 1918 did not calm the fear of revolutionary violence. Instead, Europe's turmoil seemed to be coming closer to home. Street rioting rocked the defeated German nation, threatening a Communist revolution, while the Allies sent troops to reinforce the "White" (anti-Communist) armies fighting to overthrow the Bolshevik government.

LABOR AND REVOLUTION

The Russian Revolution had begun with a strike of soldiers and industrial workers. Labor trouble was also brewing in the United States. A radical union, the Industrial Workers of the World (IWW), led several walkouts in 1918 and threatened a nationwide strike that would paralyze manufacturing and mining industries. The IWW, which called for a single nationwide union of all the country's factory and mine laborers, came short of calling for an overthrow of the U.S. government, or the establishment of a Bolshevik regime. Opponents saw their organization of workers as posing just such a threat,

**P–
R**

Justifying the Panic

The Red Scare resulted in a vast expansion of the government's powers to watch, investigate, and arrest civilians. Within the Department of Justice, a General Intelligence Division under J. Edgar Hoover collected information on thousands of suspected radicals and everyone who might be associated with them. Federal and local agents arrested thousands of individuals, denying many of them bail, legal counsel, or the right to a hearing. Attorney General A. Mitchell Palmer justified the actions of the government with a 1920 fiery editorial, "The Case Against the 'Reds'."

Like a prairie-fire, the blaze of revolution was sweeping over every American institution of law and order a year ago. It was eating its way into the homes of the American workmen, its sharp tongues of revolutionary heat were licking the altars of the churches, leaping into the belfry of the school bell, crawling into the sacred corners of American homes, seeking to replace marriage vows with libertine laws, burning up the foundations of society. . . .

My information showed that communism in this country was an organization of thousands of aliens who were direct allies of Trotzky [a Communist leader] . . . and it showed that they were making the same glittering promises of lawlessness, of criminal autocracy to Americans, that they had made to the Russian peasants. How the Department of Justice discovered upwards of 60,000 of these organized agitators of the Trotzky doctrine in the United States is the confidential information upon which the Government is now sweeping the nation clean of such alien filth. . . .

however, and believed radical foreigners leading the IWW, as well as dangerous, violent immigrants, lay at the heart of the trouble.

Inspired by the Russian Revolution, **anarchists** in the United States did commit many acts of violence. In April 1919, explosive devices were mailed to prominent politicians and business leaders, including Supreme Court Justice Oliver Wendell Holmes, banker J.P. Morgan, oil tycoon John D. Rockefeller, and Senator Thomas Hardwick of Georgia. On June 2, bombs went off in New York, Philadelphia, and Boston. In Washington, an anarchist brought a bomb to the front door of Attorney General A. Mitchell Palmer. The device exploded, killing the man who carried it and terrifying Palmer and his family. Reared as a **Quaker,** Palmer had declined an appointment as secretary of war and had stood against the arrest and prosecution of war opponents. In 1919, however, he promptly changed his stand. With the unspoken support of President Woodrow Wilson (1913–1921), Palmer ordered a nationwide sweep of suspected radicals and Socialists. The "Palmer raids" resulted in the arrest and deportation of more than 500 people.

PUBLIC SUPPORT
Palmer won support for his actions in the press. Seeking to sell newspapers, editors treated anarchism as a dire threat and one that handily replaced the now-defeated menace of the German army. The Justice Department, however, was coming under fire from opponents in the cabinet who believed that depriving legal immigrants of constitutional rights represented a violation of the government's authority. Seeking to justify his actions with an imminent national emergency, Palmer announced that he had discovered a plot to carry out a Bolshevik revolution within the United States on May 1, 1920. The day passed quietly, however, and Palmer's entire campaign against the Communists was discredited. Labor strife subsided, the country enjoyed the fruits of a booming economy, and the Red Scare died down. Isolationism, however, continued to guide the nation's foreign policy.

See also: Palmer Raids; World War I.

FURTHER READING
Finan, Chris. *From the Palmer Raids to the Patriot Act: A History of the Fight for Free Speech in America*. Boston: Beacon, 2008.

Republican Party

Formed in 1854, one of two major U.S. political parties. During the 1930s and 1940s, the Republican Party gained much of its strength from an insistence on keeping the United States isolated from world affairs.

ISOLATIONIST STANCE
After the bloodshed of World War I (1914–1918), the United States had emerged as a world power, but its people were weary of war and eager to step back from the world. They elected Republican presidents who shared their sentiment.

Warren G. Harding Elected by a landslide in 1920 for his promise that the nation would "return to normalcy" after the war, President Harding (1921–1923) quickly began imposing measures to isolate the United States from the world. He signed into law the Fordney-McCumber **tariff** on imported goods, discouraging foreign trade. He also tightened regulation of **immigration**, limiting the number of people who could relocate to the United States from foreign countries.

Calvin Coolidge After Harding's sudden death in 1923, Vice President

Calvin Coolidge (1923–1929) assumed the presidency. Coolidge's greatest legacy is the Kellogg-Briand Pact, which insisted upon "the renunciation of war as an instrument of national policy." The treaty met with little success, but provided a valuable blueprint for international law in later years.

Herbert Hoover As the **Great Depression** devastated the world economy in the early 1930s, the United States pulled its focus even further inward. In an attempt to deal with the huge economic downturn and nationwide poverty, Congress increased **tariffs,** further reducing foreign trade. President Herbert Hoover (1929–1933), however, made one significant move in regard to the nation's place in world affairs. In 1932, Hoover put forth what became known as the Stimson Doctrine, named after Secretary of State Henry Stimson. This policy, established in response to Japan's moves into China, noted that the United States would not recognize territory aggressively acquired in violation of international agreements.

NEUTRALITY ACTS
Between World War I and World War II (1939–1945), the makeup of Congress leaned Republican. Many voters viewed the party as more socially and fiscally **conservative** than the rival Democrats. The party's conservatism also was reflected in its foreign policy. It was a largely Republican Senate, led by William E. Borah and Henry Cabot Lodge, that rejected the Treaty of Versailles, thus preventing U.S. participation in the League of Nations for fear of being dragged into future conflicts following World War I.

As World War II loomed, it was again Republicans in Congress who resisted involvement, even as President Franklin D. Roosevelt (1933–1945) urged intervention. Republican senators, among them Robert La Follette, and Gerald P. Nye spoke loudly against involvement in world affairs. However, as events in Europe became increasingly chaotic, support for **nonintervention** spread beyond the Republican Party.

The Neutrality Acts, passed between 1935 and 1939, had dozens of stipulations that isolated the United States from foreign nations and overseas conflicts. With the acts, Congress established **embargoes** on trading arms and military supplies; refused loans or credit to warring nations; and kept U.S. ships out of war zones. The acts remained in place until 1941, when Roosevelt, responding to a growing catastrophe in Europe, approved the Lend-Lease Act, thus beginning a policy of aiding the war-stricken **Allies** in the fight against the Axis powers.

See also: League of Nations; Lend-Lease Act; Nye, Gerald P.; World War I; World War II.

FURTHER READING
Gould, Lewis L. *Grand Old Party: A History of the Republicans.* New York: Random House, 2003.
Lutz, Norma Jean, and Arthur M. Schlesinger. *History of the Republican Party.* New York: Chelsea House, 2000.
Reichley, A. James. *The Life of the Parties: A History of American Political Parties.* New York: The Free Press, 1992.

Reservationists

Term for U.S. senators who asked for changes to the Treaty of Versailles (1919) and the Covenant of the League of Nations before they would support it. The opposition to the treaty was led by Henry Cabot Lodge, a Republican senator from Massachusetts. Lodge, as well as Senator William E. Borah of Idaho and their followers, wanted to prevent an "entangling alliance," which they believed the League of Nations would impose on the United States. Their success in denying **ratification** of the treaty represented an important victory for **isolationists.**

Reservationists, meaning those who had reservations, or concerns, about the treaty, pointed to Article X of the covenant, which seemed to pledge the United States to direct involvement in any military conflict that may break out among league members in the future. Membership in the League of Nations directly conflicted with these senators' support of isolationism.

TACTICS

At first, Lodge fought the treaty by a tactic of delay. On July 14, he opened Senate hearings on the treaty with a word-for-word reading of the entire document, which took him two weeks. He then called a long, monotonous parade of witnesses to testify against the treaty. By the end of the hearings, the legislators and the public were growing restless, frustrated, and bored by the issue. In effect, the Lodge hearings showed President Woodrow Wilson (1913–1921) that the two-thirds majority needed to pass the treaty was doubtful, at best.

Wilson then decided to take his case directly to the people. He began a whistle-stop train tour through the country to gather support for the treaty and bring pressure on Lodge and the Senate to pass it. The stress and strain of the trip, however, ruined Wilson's health, and shortly after a speech delivered at Pueblo, Colorado, the president suffered a stroke. Partially paralyzed, he returned to Washington, D.C., now too frail to debate his opponents or carry out the normal duties of the presidency.

LODGE'S RESERVATIONS

Lodge then announced 14 reservations to the treaty, in imitation of the Fourteen Points that President Wilson had laid out for a peaceful postwar world. Lodge's key and second reservation resolved the debate over Article X:

> The United States assumes no obligation to preserve the territorial integrity or political independence of any other country or to interfere in controversies between nations—whether members of the League or not—under the provisions of Article 10. . . .

A STUBBORN PRESIDENT

Feeling he had already compromised enough, Wilson now refused to consider the reservations—partly out of stubbornness, partly due to the fact that if he accepted them the entire treaty would have to be renegotiated. In November, the treaty—with the reservations included—was defeated in the Senate. Two more Senate votes in early 1920 again rejected it. Lodge and the reservationists had won the battle. The United States rejected the Treaty of Versailles and stayed out of the League of Nations.

See also: Fourteen Points; Treaty of Versailles; World War I.

Roosevelt, Franklin D.

See Democratic Party; Lend-Lease Act; Pearl Harbor.

Russian Revolution and Civil War

Uprising in the nation of Russia and the internal strife that followed, which ultimately led to the establishment of the Union of Soviet Socialist Republics (U.S.S.R.), or Soviet Union, in 1922, a nation with a **Communist** form of government. The revolution in Russia caused widespread fear in the United States of a similar uprising and led to increased **isolationist** feelings among the population.

REVOLUTION

The **abdication** of Czar Nicholas II (1896–1917) in 1917 marked the end of the Romanov dynasty that had ruled Russia for more than 300 years. A **provisional** government took power, but in October, the radical **Bolshevik** faction of the Russian **Socialist** Party led a violent uprising in the capital of St. Petersburg. A new government was established in

Between 1732 and 1917, the Winter Palace in St. Petersburg, Russia, was the official residence of the Russian czars. The storming of the palace in 1917 became a symbol of the Russian Revolution.

January 1918, under the leadership of Vladimir I. Lenin.

The Bolsheviks immediately began peace negotiations with Germany, ending Russian participation in World War I (1914–1918). Under the terms of the Treaty of Brest-Litovsk, signed in March 1918, Russia withdrew from the war and gave up its western territories to Germany. Those opposing the Bolsheviks used the treaty as a rallying point. They gathered supporters of the czar to fight for the restoration of the monarchy and the overthrow of the Bolsheviks. This set the stage for a long civil war that would draw several nations into the fighting.

COMMUNIST FORCES

Under the Communist leader Leon Trotsky, the Bolsheviks organized the Red Army to fight for control of Russia against the counterrevolutionary forces, known as the White Army. While the Bolsheviks centered their forces on the cities of Moscow and St. Petersburg, the different parts of the White Army were spread around the country. The White forces controlled several key ports and railways, but communications across the vast Russian nation were difficult, and the scattering of forces made their military offensives impossible to coordinate.

In the meantime, a 40,000-strong Czech Legion, made up of former prisoners of war, fought its way east through Siberia—the vast forested region of eastern Russia. Operating with the scattered White forces, the Czech Legion drove Bolshevik armies out of much of eastern Siberia.

ALLIED SUPPORT OF THE WHITE ARMY

The United States and its allies greatly feared the threat of Bolshevik revolution spreading to the rest of Europe. The Allies were also determined to bring Russia back into the war against Germany and to ensure Russia's repayment of a large war debt owed to Western banks. This prompted the British and French to send troops to join the White Army. The British landed forces at Murmansk in northwestern Russia, and the French sent forces to Odessa, a port on the Black Sea.

The British and the French persuaded President Woodrow Wilson (1913–1921) to join this effort. Wilson, despite opposition in the War Department, agreed, and in July 1918, a force of 5,000 U.S. troops landed at Archangel, a far northern port on Russia's border with Finland. Another 8,000 troops mustered in California and the Philippines and landed at Vladivostok, a Russian port on the Pacific.

Intervention in the Russian Civil War provoked strong protests at home. Many Americans believed the United States had no vital interests in Russia and had no business fighting in support of the Russian monarchy. Wilson, however, believed that U.S. intervention might spur Germany to divert troops back to the eastern front in Russia. If the Bolsheviks were defeated, the United States could count on the repayment of war debts. The United States would also be protecting war material already sent to Russia and that was now stored in warehouses along the Trans-Siberian Railway and in the port of Murmansk.

By 1922, however, the Bolsheviks were firmly in control of Russia. The failure to turn back the Russian Revolution gave strength to the isolationists: The United States should remain neutral in any future European conflict.

See also: Japan; World War I.

FURTHER READING

Bullock, David. *The Russian Civil War, 1918–1921.* London: Osprey Publishing, 2008.

Mawdsley, Evan. *Russian Civil War.* New York: Pegasus, 2009.

S–T

Smoot-Hawley Tariff

Law passed by Congress in June 1930 that set high **tariffs** on goods imported into the United States. The law reflected the **isolationist** feelings of many Americans. The high tariffs established under this law prevented many foreign companies from selling their products in the United States and led to retaliation by the nation's trading partners. Many economists believe that the drop in foreign trade worsened the effects of the **Great Depression** of the 1930s.

PROTECTING AMERICAN BUSINESS

Senator Reed Smoot of Utah and Senator Willis Hawley of Oregon, both Republicans, sponsored the law in Congress. Smoot, a prominent supporter of tariffs, had been a key supporter of the Fordney-McCumber Act, which raised tariffs to the highest level in U.S. history in 1922. Since that time, the Republican Party had generally been in support of **protectionism,** while the Democrats—then the minority party—opposed them.

Those supporting high tariffs believed they would solve the problem of competition from foreign nations. They believed that cheap goods from abroad, where labor costs were lower, were driving down prices and putting many U.S. farmers and companies out of business. It was thought that the Smoot-Hawley Tariff would help support prices for American farm goods and help industries to prosper from a more controlled market for their products. As a result, it was believed, unemployment would fall and wages would rise for American workers.

ISOLATIONIST SUPPORT

Isolationists in the United States also generally supported the bill, as they had the Fordney-McCumber Act of 1922. In their view, protecting U.S. companies from foreign competition was an important part of keeping European conflicts and entanglements at bay.

Specific Tax Rates Smoot-Hawley imposed specific rates on units of production, rather than taxing a percentage of the value of these products. Importing pig iron—a type of iron with a high carbon content—into the United States, for example, now cost $1.125 a ton (no matter what the pig iron was worth). As the value of products declined during the Great

Depression, the tariff rose as a percentage of their value. The result was that importing goods to the United States became increasingly costly.

Some Industries Benefit Certain industries, of course, did benefit from a captive market in the United States. Sugar producers, for example, no longer had to compete with imports from Cuba and other producers in Latin America, as Smoot-Hawley imposed a tax equal to more than 75 percent of the value of imported sugar (an important reason for the support of Smoot-Hawley by Democratic legislators from Florida, where sugar was an important crop). Producers of tobacco, cotton, lumber, wool, paper, and flax also benefited.

FOREIGN REACTION
Supporters of the Smoot-Hawley Tariff, however, did not count on retaliation by foreign nations, many of them with large, state-controlled industries. In such economies, governments often control production and prices as well as customs duties. It was a relatively simple matter for these nations to restrict or ban imports from the United States. In the face of rising unemployment around the world, a global trade war resulted. U.S. allies and trading partners raised their own barriers while struggling to protect their own industries and fight a rising tide of unemployment.

Smoot-Hawley came under fire even before it was passed. Leading bankers and industrialists opposed the bill and then demanded that Congress repeal it once it had taken effect. Canada, France, and Britain raised tariffs, while Germany strived

for complete self-sufficiency. Imports and exports in the United States fell by more than half, as did the country's **gross national product (GNP)**. Unemployment hit 25 percent in 1933, the worst year of the Great Depression.

Signed into law by President Herbert Hoover (1929–1933), Smoot-Hawley was strongly opposed by his successor, President Franklin D. Roosevelt (1933–1945). The high tariffs imposed by the Smoot-Hawley Tariff Act were gradually reduced, while Congress passed the Reciprocal Trade Agreements Act in 1934. With this law and international trade agreements signed in the wake of World War II (1939–1945), the United States became a champion of free global trade.

See also: Democratic Party; Republican Party; Thomas, Norman; War Reparations.

FURTHER READING
Shlaes, Amity. *The Forgotten Man: A New History of the Great Depression.* New York: Harper Perennial, 2008.

S–T

Thomas, Norman (1884–1968)

American politician, minister, **pacifist**, and member of the Socialist Party. Norman Thomas was an outspoken critic of the United States' entry into World War I (1914–1918) and strongly supported isolationism during the 1920s and 1930s. After the Japanese attack on Pearl Harbor, Hawaii, in December 1941, he supported U.S. entry into World War II (1939–1945) as a just cause.

CAREER AS A MINISTER

In 1911, Thomas graduated from seminary and was ordained a Presbyterian minister. He went to work in East Harlem, a poor area of New York City, becoming pastor of the East Harlem Presbyterian Church. Thomas's religious training had exposed him to the Social Gospel movement popular in Protestant faiths in the nineteenth and twentieth centuries. The movement stressed viewing social ills, such as poverty, from a religious perspective, spurring people to action by appealing to their beliefs that helping the poor and the sick was doing God's work.

At the same time, Thomas was also developing a pacifist stance. He opposed U.S. involvement in World War I because it did not appear to him to be a war with a clear moral victor. He felt that the United States' biggest interest in World War I was economic, which was not reason enough to send young men off to die. Because religion no longer appeared to be a method to change people's lives for the better, Thomas began looking elsewhere.

MOVE INTO POLITICS

In 1921, Thomas became editor of *The Nation*, a Socialist paper. In 1922, he became codirector of the League for Industrial Democracy, a political action group whose purpose was to educate people about the goals of Socialism. Thomas was also a founding member of the American Civil Liberties Union (ACLU).

In 1928, Thomas became the Socialist Party's nominee for president. While he never received many votes, Thomas always presented himself well and gave intelligent speeches. People respected his views, even if they were not going to elect him president. He spoke often of the difference between Socialism and Communism, a refrain he took up again when the United States entered the Cold War in the years after World War II.

Initially, Thomas was as opposed to participating in World War II as he had been to participating in World War I. However, following the Japanese attack on Pearl Harbor, Hawaii, Thomas changed his position. It had become clear to him that World War II was a substantially different conflict and that Nazi Germany posed a greater threat to the world than he had previously thought.

Thomas's later years were spent supporting various **progressive** causes. He supported efforts toward international peace. He continued to speak out against hypocrisy within the church. Thomas died on December 19, 1968.

See also: America First Committee; World War I; World War II.

FURTHER READING
Gregory, Raymond F. *Norman Thomas: The Great Dissenter.* New York: Algora Publishing, 2008.

Treaty of Versailles (1919)

Agreement signed in Paris in 1919 that formally ended World War I (1914–1918). In 1920, however, the treaty was rejected by the U.S. Senate, which must **ratify** all international treaties before they take effect under U.S. law. Because the Senate did not approve the treaty, the United States did not join the League of Nations, which was a part of the treaty. Thus, rejection of the treaty furthered the nation's **isolationist** foreign policy.

END OF THE FIGHTING

After four years of war in northern France, an offensive by the **Allies**, including Great Britain, France, and the United States, drove the German armies in retreat toward the Rhine River. With Germany's military and industry exhausted, German officers asked for an **armistice**, which was signed at the forest of Compiègne, north of Paris, on November 11, 1918.

Diplomats sign the Treaty of Versailles at a ceremony in the Hall of Mirrors, in July 1919, as painted by Sir William Orpen. The treaty did not win acceptance by the U.S. Senate, despite President Woodrow Wilson's (center) strenuous efforts, nor did it prevent another global conflict.

Meeting in Paris The major Allied powers—Great Britain, France, Italy, and the United States—first gathered in Paris in January 1919 to discuss the terms of the peace treaty. Since the armistice, President Woodrow Wilson (1913–1921) had declared his aim of writing a treaty to ensure global peace and security and following the Fourteen Points, a set of principles created by a committee of American scholars and politicians during the war. Wilson believed that the United States could now serve as a mediator in the conflicts that had long plagued Europe.

Wilson Arrives in Paris On his arrival, Wilson was hailed by the French populace, both for the entry of the United States into the war in April 1917 and for his determination to conclude a lasting peace in Europe. Despite this idealistic goal, the talks in Paris soon became a hard-fought negotiation over the spoils of war. Nations large and small sent diplomats to Paris to argue over territory, money, and the right to govern ethnic minorities living within their borders. Diplomats from the losing nations—Austria, Hungary, and Germany—were shut out of the negotiations and given no say whatsoever in the final terms of the treaty.

CONFLICTING GOALS

Each of the Allies brought different goals to the negotiating table. France sought to regain Alsace-Lorraine, a territory lost to Germany during the Franco-Prussian War (1870–1871). French diplomats also wanted to permanently weaken the German military and to prevent the Germans from ever threatening another invasion. To this end, the French and British wanted to impose a harsh punishment on Germany in the form of enormous war **reparations**.

Italy wanted control of Fiume, a port on the Adriatic Sea then under the control of Austria. The British sought to maintain their control over a far-flung colonial empire that included nations—such as India—that had fought on the side of the Allies. The United States wanted to ensure the repayment of war debts and keep the United States free from any future conflicts and entanglements on the European continent. In the months of haggling, demands, and declarations, Wilson's principles and the Fourteen Points were largely forgotten.

Although German diplomats were present at the Paris negotiations, they were given no say in the discussions. When the final terms of the peace were resolved in June, they were simply told to sign, under threat of an invasion by the Allies. The armistice at Compiègne and the Treaty of Versailles inspired a bitter resentment among the German population, which later allowed Adolf Hitler

(1933–1945) to rouse German voters to his side.

TERMS OF THE TREATY

The result of the Paris negotiations was the Treaty of Versailles, formally signed at the royal French palace of Versailles on June 28, 1919. The treaty ran more than 200 pages long and contained 440 articles. Under the terms of the treaty, Germany accepted complete responsibility for the war. The treaty held Kaiser Wilhelm II (1888–1918), the emperor of Germany, to be a war criminal, subject to arrest and trial. (The kaiser, however, had fled to Holland at the end of the war.) Germany also surrendered Alsace-Lorraine to France and lost all its overseas colonies.

The treaty limited the German army to 100,000 troops and banned **conscription**. Germany could not produce or import war material, and its navy was limited to 10,000 crew and 30 ships, to include 6 battleships. German forces were forbidden from entering the Rhineland, the country's most important industrial region, which would be occupied by troops from France and Belgium. The Rhineland was to remain "demilitarized" for at least 15 years.

A large swath of eastern Germany and the Baltic Sea port of Danzig were surrendered to the re-created nation of Poland. This created the "Polish corridor," a narrow strip of land that separated Germany from the German province of East Prussia. It placed 7 million ethnic Germans under the government of Poland, which was revived after more than a century of division and occupation by Germany, Austria, and Russia. Germany also lost territory to Belgium, Denmark, and Czechoslovakia and was expressly forbidden to unite with Austria.

Creating the League of Nations The treaty also created the League of Nations, which, it was hoped, would resolve future disputes before they became wars. By the Covenant of the League of Nations, each member had the responsibility to intervene, where necessary, to help resolve these disputes and arrive at a just settlement of grievances. On returning home, President Wilson came up against strong opposition to this treaty provision. Led by Henry Cabot Lodge of Massachusetts and other Republican senators, these "reservationists" would not vote to ratify the Treaty of Versailles unless major changes were made.

TREATY EFFECTS

Although he made a heroic effort to win public support for the Treaty of Versailles, President Wilson could not overcome opposition in the Senate. When presented with a chance to negotiate with Senator Henry Cabot Lodge and other treaty opponents, Wilson stubbornly refused. Lodge, although not an isolationist, did not want to see the United States dragged into another foreign conflict where the country had no vital national interests—and he believed that the Covenant of the League of Nations, with its guarantee of mutual aid and protection, would do just that.

Unable to reconcile opponents of the league, Wilson saw the treaty fail in the U.S. Senate. As a result, although the United States had signed the treaty in Paris, it remained unratified, and the country did not formally join the League of Nations.

REPARATIONS AND RESENTMENT

In the meantime, reparations to be paid by Germany were set by an Allied Reparations Committee, which eventually arrived at a figure of 226 billion gold marks. This was far beyond the resources of the German government, which soon fell behind on its payments.

Without money for investment and repair of its industry, Germany took the fatal step of simply increasing its money supply. The German mark quickly lost its value, and **hyperinflation** destroyed the savings of ordinary German workers. The economic chaos increased resentment of the Versailles Treaty in Germany, and Adolf Hitler's promise to renounce the treaty and return Germany to its former military glory found growing acceptance. In his memoir, *Mein Kampf,* Hitler made his opinion of the treaty and his future intentions clear:

> What a use could be made of the Treaty of Versailles! . . . How each one of the points of that Treaty could be branded in the minds and hearts of the German people until sixty million men and women find their souls aflame with a feeling of rage and shame; and a torrent of fire bursts forth as from a furnace, and a will of steel is forced from it, with the common cry: "Wir wollen wieder Waffen!—We will have arms again!"

History Speaks

Establishing the League

Signed in June 1920, the diplomats who drafted the Treaty of Versailles set out the full consequences of World War I for Germany and the rules of conduct for nations in the future. The treaty began with the Covenant of the League of Nations.

THE HIGH CONTRACTING PARTIES, In order to promote international co-operation and to achieve international peace and security by the acceptance of obligations not to resort to war . . . Agree to this Covenant of the League of Nations.

ARTICLE 1. The original Members of the League of Nations shall be those of the Signatories which are named in the Annex to this Covenant and also such of those other States named in the Annex as shall accede without reservation to this Covenant.

ARTICLE 2. The action of the League under this Covenant shall be effected through the instrumentality of an Assembly and of a Council, with a permanent Secretariat.

ARTICLE 3. The Assembly shall consist of Representatives of the Members of the League. The Assembly shall meet at stated intervals and from time to time as occasion may require . . .

ARTICLE 4. The Council shall consist of Representatives of

After his Nazi party won a general election, Hitler became Germany's head of state in January 1933. Within a short time, he began to defy the terms of the Treaty of Versailles, with the full support of the German military and a majority of the German population. Germany began conscripting men into its armed forces in 1935. In the next year, German troops entered the Rhineland, in direct violation of the treaty, and in 1938, Germany **annexed** Austria and the Sudetenland, a region of western Czechoslovakia with a large population of ethnic Germans. Rather than a military confrontation, the leaders of Britain and France chose appeasement of Hitler and conciliation with Germany's demands. In September 1939, Hitler invaded Poland, claiming to seek a reunification of Germany with East Prussia, even as his armies drove directly east toward Warsaw, the Polish capital. This event touched off World War II (1939–1945) in Europe.

FAILURE

As a result of these events, historians view the Treaty of Versailles as a failure and an important cause of World War II. In their attempt to ensure a the Principal Allied and Associated Powers. . . . The Council may deal at its meetings with any matter within the sphere of action of the League or affecting the peace of the world . . .

ARTICLE 5. Except where otherwise expressly provided in this Covenant or by the terms of the present Treaty, decisions at any meeting of the Assembly or of the Council shall require the agreement of all the Members of the League represented at the meeting. . . .

ARTICLE 6. The permanent Secretariat shall be established at the Seat of the League . . .

ARTICLE 7. The Seat of the League is established at Geneva . . .

ARTICLE 8. The Members of the League recognise that the maintenance of peace requires the reduction of national armaments . . . The Members of the League undertake to interchange full and frank information as to the scale of their armaments, their military, naval, and air programmes and the condition of such of their industries as are adaptable to war-like purposes.

ARTICLE 9. A permanent Commission shall be constituted to advise the Council on the execution of the provisions of Articles 1 and 8. . . .

ARTICLE 10. The Members of the League undertake to respect and preserve as against external aggression the territorial integrity and existing political independence of all Members of the League. In case of any such aggression or in case of any threat or danger of such aggression the Council shall advise upon the means by which this obligation shall be fulfilled.

S–T

lasting peace, the Allies at the Paris negotiations tried to ensure perpetual German weakness, both economic and military. The effect was to raise German resentment to such a point that a tyrant handily won a **democratic** election, setting the country and the rest of the world on course for another catastrophic war—World War II. The entry of the United States into World War II ended the nation's isolationist foreign policy.

See also: Fourteen Points; France; Great Britain; War Reparations; World War I; World War II.

FURTHER READING

Brezina, Corona. *The Treaty of Versailles, 1919: A Primary Source Examination of the Treaty That Ended World War I.* New York: Rosen, 2006.

Hay, Jeff. *The Treaty of Versailles.* San Diego, Calif.: Greenhaven Press, 2002.

Macmillan, Margaret. *Paris 1919: Six Months That Changed the World.* New York: Random House, 2003.

Tripartite Pact

See Axis Powers.

Triple Entente

See Great Britain; France.

W-Y

War Reparations

Payments made to make amends for loss of life and property in wartime. After the **armistice** of 1918, following World War I (1914–1918), the victorious Allies proclaimed Germany to be at fault for starting the war and demanded heavy **reparations** be made by Germany as a part of any final settlement. Many believe that the harsh reparations led to the anger of the German people and ultimately to the rise of the Nazi dictator Adolf Hitler (1933–1945).

Hitler's aggressive and **nationalistic** policies led to the outbreak of World War II (1939–1945) in 1939. The entry of the United States into World War II in 1941 ended the nation's **isolationist** foreign policy.

DETERMINING THE AMOUNT TO PAY

The Paris Peace Conference produced the Treaty of Versailles, but no agreement on the amount of money Germany would have to pay or the time Germany would have to pay it. A Reparations Commission convened to determine this final important point. In early 1921, two years after the Treaty of Versailles was signed, the commission arrived at the figure of 132 billion German gold marks (currency backed by an equivalent value of gold), or $31.5 billion. Gold marks ensured that inflation, which lowered the value of ordinary currency, would not also lower the value of the reparations payments.

With its economy failing after the war, Germany struggled to meet the reparations bill until January 1923, when it defaulted, or stopped making payments. In reprisal, the governments of France and Belgium ordered troops into the Ruhr, the industrial heartland of Germany. The occupation did nothing to resolve the problem, however. While the German economy was collapsing and **hyperinflation** destroyed its currency, the government lost most of the tax income that allowed payments to be made.

WAR DEBT AND ISOLATIONISM

The issue of reparations and outstanding war debt bolstered the isolationist cause in the United States. During the war, the United States had loaned 17 different nations more than $10 billion for war equipment. War debts became a bitter and divisive issue between the United States, Great Britain, and France and complicated the negotiations over German reparations. The spectacle of former allies fighting over debts and money showed the futility of entangling the United States in the affairs of Europe—just as President George Washington (1789–1797) had warned in his famous 1796 Farewell Address.

Dawes Plan In 1924, U.S. banker and Vice President Charles G. Dawes was appointed head of a committee to work out the problem of German reparations. The Dawes Plan reduced the outstanding payments, giving

Germany more time to pay while, hopefully, its economy improved. Germany adopted a new currency, and France and Belgium withdrew their troops from the Ruhr. When the stream of loans slowed in 1928, Germany found itself again unable to meet its payments.

Young Plan As the Dawes Plan did no better in getting the reparations from Germany, a new committee formed in 1929 under banker Owen D. Young. The Young Plan reduced the total reparations debt and gave Germany 58 years to pay it. With the crash of the stock market in October 1929 and the **Great Depression** that followed, the Young Plan had no more chance of success than the Dawes Plan.

Although the U.S. Senate had rejected the Treaty of Versailles, the United States remained closely involved with Europe and its conflicts through the Young and Dawes plans and the issue of war reparations. Despite these U.S. diplomatic moves, the nation remained firmly isolationist in its foreign policy through the 1920s and 1930s.

See also: Dawes Plan; Treaty of Versailles; World War I; World War II; Young Plan.

FURTHER READING

Kent, Bruce. *The Spoils of War: The Politics, Economics, and Diplomacy of Reparations 1918–1932.* New York: Oxford University Press, 1992.

Taylor, A.J.P. *The Origins of the Second World War.* New York: Simon and Schuster, 1996.

Washington's Farewell Address

Speech by President George Washington (1789–1797) published in the pages of the *American Daily Advertiser* on September 19, 1796. Washington never actually gave the speech in public. In his Farewell Address, Washington expressed the opinion that the United States should avoid involvement in European affairs and conflicts. This point was often cited by **isolationists** of the twentieth century to support their view that the country should, as much as possible, avoid entanglement with the world beyond its shores.

POLITICAL VIEWS

The American **republic** of Washington's day was an experiment in modern government. European nations were still under the control of **monarchs** and a class of wealthy landowners. They provided few guideposts for a nation founded on a written constitution and based on **democracy**, free speech, and property rights held in common. Washington, already known as the father of the country, and other public figures constantly debated the best way for the nation to preserve its ideals, liberty, and prosperity. The Farewell Address was Washington's summation of what he had learned and his attempt to give the nation some caring advice.

Washington placed foreign affairs at the end of the address. He saw danger in excessive hatred or fondness for foreign nations, warning that it often led to "frequent collisions, obstinate, envenomed, and bloody contests." He advised his readers to avoid foreign influences, as they often led leaders astray in looking after the nation's own interests. The nation had an obligation, of course, to live up to its promises to other countries. However, "So far as we have already formed engagements, let them be fulfilled with perfect good faith. Here let us stop."

IDEAL LOCATION

Its physical isolation from Europe, in Washington's opinion, gave the United States an advantage in shaping its own future. It allowed the nation to grow prosperous from its seemingly unlimited land and resources and the labor of new **immigrants.** It protected the nation from foreign invasion and allowed its leaders to choose their battles wisely. "Why forgo the advantages of so peculiar a situation," Washington asked. "Why ... entangle our peace and prosperity in the toils of European ambition, rivalship [sic], interest, humor, or caprice?"

WASHINGTON'S ADVICE

Washington concluded his argument with a phrase cited by isolationists for the next two centuries:

It is our true policy to steer clear of permanent alliances with any portion of the foreign world.

This isolationist philosophy was followed throughout the nineteenth century by American leaders who saw Washington as a national icon of wisdom and virtue. As the nation grew and prospered, however, Americans found their interests often colliding with those of foreign nations and the U.S. economy tied increasingly to the wealth and resources of Europe, Asia, and Latin America. By the middle of the twentieth century, avoiding "entangling alliances" with the outside world was no longer an option.

See also: Fourteen Points; Pearl Harbor; World War I.

FURTHER READING

Ferling, John. *The Ascent of George Washington: The Hidden Political Genius of an American Icon.* London: Bloomsbury Press, 2009.

Spalding, Matthew. *A Sacred Union of Citizens: George Washington's Farewell Address and the American Character.* Lanham, Md.: Rowman and Littlefield, 1998.

Wilson, Woodrow (1856–1924)

Twenty-eighth president of the United States; Woodrow Wilson led the country into World War I (1914–1918). Wilson tried to keep the nation out of the war, but in 1917, he finally asked Congress to declare war on the Central powers. Wilson was an idealist who helped to found the League of Nations to preserve world peace, but he could not get his own country to join it. Thus, after the U.S. Senate rejected the Treaty of Versailles that Wilson helped negotiate, the country's traditional **isolationist** foreign policy returned to favor.

EARLY LIFE

Woodrow Wilson was born on December 28, 1856, in Staunton, Virginia. His father was a Presbyterian minister, and the family moved often. The Wilsons were in Augusta, Georgia, during the Civil War (1861–1865), when Wilson's father's church was made into a hospital. As a young boy, Woodrow witnessed the horrors of war, which had a lasting effect on him.

Wilson had difficulty as a student. He began his formal studies at age nine and could not read until two years later. He was always a slow reader, despite developing an interest in literature. Some historians attribute his reading difficulty to dyslexia, a learning disability. Others point to the poor state of education in the South during the **Reconstruction** era after the Civil War.

Wilson briefly attended Davidson College in North Carolina before being accepted to what is now Princeton University in 1875. While at Princeton, Wilson became editor of the school paper. He read avidly and led an active and successful academic life. He graduated from Princeton in 1879 and went on to study law at the University of Virginia.

BACK TO THE UNIVERSITY

In 1882, Wilson earned his law degree and passed the bar exam. He spent two years practicing law but found the profession unfulfilling. Instead, he went back to school, enrolling as a graduate student at Johns Hopkins University. In 1886, he earned a Ph.D. in history and political science—the only American president to have a doctorate.

Wilson taught at Bryn Mawr and Wesleyan colleges before landing a position at Princeton University. His teaching career flourished. Wilson became the highest-paid professor on staff and president of the university in 1902.

GOVERNOR OF NEW JERSEY

In 1910, Wilson left Princeton to successfully run for governor of New Jersey as the Democratic candidate. As governor, Wilson implemented a number of **progressive** changes. He instituted campaign finance reform and fought against the party boss system by instituting primary elections. Wilson also introduced New Jersey's workers' compensation system, which granted benefits to injured workers. These reforms gave Wilson substantial ground on which to run for national office.

PRESIDENT

In 1912, Wilson ran against former Republican president Theodore Roosevelt (1901–1909) and **incumbent** Republican president William Howard Taft (1909–1913). Because the Republican voters were split between Roosevelt and Taft, Wilson won the election. Wilson's plan for the country was called New Freedom and, despite being from the opposite party of the previous two presidents, continued many of their reform policies.

New Freedom Policies New Freedom called for lower **tariffs,** a progressive Republican stance that Taft had abandoned, laws curtailing abusive business practices by large corporations, and banking reform. Wilson's skill as a speaker helped forward these reforms. Unlike presidents before him, Wilson conducted himself much like a British prime minister. He appeared personally before Congress, the first president to do so since John Adams (1797–1801), to secure legislative support for an agenda that he had prepared before entering the White House.

New Reforms To ensure that his reforms were passed, Wilson also kept Congress in session for nearly a year and a half. This was unprecedented, but his strategy worked. Among the legislation Wilson passed was the Underwood-Simmons Tariff, lowering tariffs for the first time in 40 years. He also created the Federal Reserve System to give the government more control over the economy. The Clayton Antitrust Act put restrictions on business and strengthened the ability of labor unions to fight for fair working conditions. He also created the Federal Trade Commission (FTC) to oversee businesses.

In addition to these reforms, Wilson also signed legislation that limited railroad workers to eight-hour work days, that abolished child labor, and that granted government loans to farmers. Many progressive Republicans were drawn to his side. These reforms are especially notable because the balance of power in Congress had shifted away from the Democrats in 1914.

WILSON'S FOREIGN POLICY
While Wilson's domestic policies were successful, his foreign affairs policies proved less so. World War I began in Europe in 1914. Wilson was an isolationist at the time, striving to remain **neutral,** at least when it came to the war in Europe.

Western Hemisphere On the other hand, the United States participated in a number of military actions in Latin America. U.S. forces invaded Haiti and the Dominican Republic. In 1916, American troops attempted to hunt down Pancho Villa, a Mexican revolutionary who sent raiding parties across the border into New Mexico.

Neutrality The United States officially remained nonaligned in World War I until the 1915 sinking of the *Lusitania*, a British passenger liner, by German submarines. One hundred and twenty-eight U.S. passengers died, and the country wanted revenge. At first, Wilson pursued peace and asked the Germans to cease their submarine attacks. For their own reasons, the Germans did limit their attacks, and the United States maintained its distance from the war throughout 1916.

In 1917, after winning reelection, Wilson attempted to end World War I by offering to mediate peace. He asked warring nations what their terms for peace would be and pledged to help create a "league of nations" in which grievances could be aired and resolutions reached without the need for war.

War! His efforts were in vain. The Germans returned to submarine warfare on February 1. In addition, British intelligence intercepted a telegram, known as the Zimmermann telegram, from the German ambassador in the

United States to the German ambassador in Mexico detailing a plan to foment war between Mexico and the United States. In the face of such provocation, and with the public outcry over the *Lusitania* sinking, Wilson had no choice but to ask Congress to declare war.

PEACE AT LAST

A year and a half after the United States joined World War I, the Germans sued for peace. On the eleventh hour of the eleventh day of the eleventh month of 1918, the war was declared over. His popularity at a peak in the United States and Europe, Wilson saw an opportunity to bring the world a just and lasting peace. With this goal in mind, he traveled to France to attend the Paris Peace Conference.

Wilson's idealism was made plain in his Fourteen Points, revealed in a speech given to Congress on January 8, 1918. Wilson had hoped that the peace treaty would be based on the Fourteen Points. The resulting Treaty of Versailles, however, was not what he had hoped for. Seeking to punish Germany for starting the war, the **Allies** imposed heavy reparations on the country. In addition, Germany lost all of its overseas colonies. The terms of the treaty were far harsher on Germany than either Wilson or the Germans had originally been led to believe. The treaty also established the League of Nations, and redrew the map of eastern Europe, creating the countries of Poland, Czechoslovakia, and Yugoslavia, among others. Wilson returned to the United States

believing that once the League of Nations was in place conflicts could be resolved, thus leading to lasting peace.

The peace conference had been a great strain on Wilson's health. When he returned to the United States, he found little time for rest. Republicans in the Senate, fearful of obligations imposed by the League of Nations, would not **ratify** the Treaty of Versailles. In an attempt to secure its passage, Wilson toured the country, giving 39 speeches in support of the treaty in three weeks.

OPPOSITION TO THE TREATY

Senator Henry Cabot Lodge of Massachusetts was a major opponent of the Treaty of Versailles. Lodge's greatest fear was that joining the League of Nations would hand over too much of the United States' independence to foreign powers. He did not want the U.S. military to be required to participate in actions where the country had no vital interests to protect.

As chair of the Foreign Relations Committee in the Senate, Lodge had the power to delay a vote on the treaty. This gave him and other opponents of the League of Nations a chance to sway public opinion. Further, Lodge introduced **amendments** to the treaty that undermined its intent. Wilson would not support any such amendments.

The campaign against Lodge and other isolationists further strained Wilson's failing health. On September 25, 1919, he nearly had a nervous breakdown, and on October 2, he suffered a stroke that left him partially

W– Y

paralyzed. The Senate never ratified the treaty, and Wilson never fully recovered from his stroke.

In the 1920 election, Republicans won a sweeping victory, winning the presidency and majorities in both houses of Congress. They took the win as proof that the country rejected Wilson's progressivism and stance in international politics. Wilson died in his home on February 3, 1924, still believing that an international governing body could have prevented future war.

See also: Borah, William E.; Central Powers; Democratic Party; Fourteen Points; League of Nations; Lodge, Henry Cabot; Treaty of Versailles; World War I.

FURTHER READING

Brands, H.W., and Arthur M. Schlesinger. *Woodrow Wilson*. New York: Times Books, 2003.

World War I (1914–1918)

Worldwide conflict that started in Europe in 1914 and which caused the United States to abandon its long-held foreign policy of isolationism. After the war, however, the United States once again resumed its **isolationist** worldview, refusing to join the newly formed League of Nations and passing a series of Neutrality Acts designed to prevent entanglement in foreign affairs.

BACKGROUND

During the 1880s, the European powers of Germany, Austria-Hungary, and Italy formed the Triple Alliance. In turn, Great Britain and France formed an alliance that became known as the Triple Entente after Russia joined in 1907. Later, Italy changed sides, associating itself with the Entente instead of the Alliance. These blocs, or groups, established a balance of power that seemed to avoid war.

Conflicts Filled with **nationalistic** spirit, each of the great powers worked to win superiority in Europe and, at the same time, protect itself from the other powers. Each also sought advantage in Africa, Asia, and the Pacific Region. Each nation acquired colonies for trade, raw materials, and military bases. Colonies brought prestige to a nation and profits to businesses. The great powers also needed military strength.

Great Britain had the largest navy, but Germany raced to equal or excel it. France, Germany, and Russia all had huge armies based on **conscription,** but none could allow another to get too far ahead. In fear of falling behind, each nation increased the size of its armed forces, and thus increased the threat to all. Each nation hoped to keep the balance of power on its side, but none could be certain that it was.

ASSASSINATION OF THE ARCHDUKE

On June 28, 1914, a young Serbian nationalist shot and killed Archduke Franz Ferdinand, the heir to the Austro-Hungarian throne, also killing the archduke's pregnant wife. The assassination took place in Sarajevo—a town in the Austrian province of Bosnia.

The assassin, Gavrilo Princep, wanted Serbia to be free from Austrian rule. Fearful that Austria would continue to keep the Serbs and other Slavic peoples in its empire, Princep and other Serbian nationalists plotted and carried out the assassination, although local Serbian governmental officials knew about the plot and could have prevented the killing.

At the time of the assassination, few people expected a major war to result, but the minor incident quickly sparked worldwide fighting. Leading diplomats from the major powers desperately tried to stop the rush to war, but their efforts were in vain. All of them held national aims for power and prestige that could not be settled peacefully.

DECLARATIONS OF WAR

On July 23, 1914, Austria-Hungary sent an ultimatum to Serbia which, if accepted, would have humiliated Serbia and given Austria-Hungary dominance in the Balkans. At the same time, Germany promised Austria-Hungary its full support, while Russia pledged to stand behind Serbia.

Serbia rejected the demands of the ultimatum, and on July 28, Austria-Hungary declared war on Serbia and found itself at war with Russia as well. France, in turn, supported Russia, while Germany, fulfilling its promise, backed Austria-Hungary. When Germany invaded Belgium to invade France, Great Britain joined France and Russia. Later, Italy and most of the small nations of Europe were either involved or entered the war on their own.

U.S. REACTION

Immediately after the outbreak of the war, President Woodrow Wilson (1913–1921) issued a proclamation of **neutrality.** He urged Americans to be "impartial in thought as well as action." At first, this seemed possible. It soon became clear, however, that the citizens of the United States could not remain "impartial in thought."

The United States was a nation of immigrants and children of immigrants from all over Europe. In 1914, more than 32 million people living in the United States were either immigrants or had a father or mother who was. Most Americans, with their traditions and language from Britain, favored the **Allies,** especially after the German invasion of Belgium. Yet each immigrant group tended to favor the land of its origin, and public opinion was sharply divided.

Allied Powers in World War I*	
Major Powers	**Minor Powers**
Great Britain	Serbia
France	Belgium
Italy	Portugal
Russia	Greece
United States	Romania
Japan	

*Other nations also joined the Allies but did not send troops into battle.

U.S. INVOLVEMENT

The leaders of the warring nations believed that the war would be short. They were mistaken, for after the initial battles of movement, the armies settled down to four long years of

W–
Y

desperate **trench warfare.** Soon, the warring powers needed more goods of every kind than their own industries and farms could supply. Because the United States had great agricultural and industrial power, the products from its farms and factories could decide the outcome of the war.

Food and Materials Because supplies from the United States could be decisive in the war effort, each of the alliances not only attempted to get as much as they could but also to prevent such supplies from reaching their enemies. Great Britain, with its huge navy, blockaded German ports and controlled the imports of nations bordering Germany. In doing so, they frequently violated international law, but while they confiscated property, they took few lives and did little to alienate American public opinion. Thus, most Americans were sympathetic to the Allies.

To overcome the power of the British navy, Germany resorted to a new weapon—the submarine. By sinking supply ships headed to Britain and France, German naval leaders believed they could reduce the flow of food and war materials across the Atlantic. Deprived of these essential goods, the Allies could not effectively continue the war.

Submarine Warfare Early in 1915, Germany declared that it would sink on sight every enemy merchant ship sailing within a certain zone around Great Britain. The Germans warned American ships to stay out of that area. President Wilson protested, but with little result. In May, off the coast of Ireland, a German submarine sank the British liner *Lusitania,* causing the loss of nearly 1,200 lives, including 128 Americans.

Some Americans demanded war, but Wilson knew that the majority of the people still opposed the nation's entry into the conflict. Wilson protested to the German government, but German submarines continued to sink ships. However, after a submarine torpedoed the French ship *Sussex* in spring 1916, the Germans agreed to stop sinking ships on sight. U.S. entry into the war was forestalled for a time. Yet, public opinion swung more and more toward the Allies.

WAR!

After his reelection to a second term in November 1916, President Wilson again tried to mediate an end to the war. In January 1917, however, the German government announced that it would resume its use of unrestricted submarine warfare. In response, Wilson ordered the arming of all American merchant vessels—hoping to convince the German government to change its policy, without success.

In March, the American press announced that the British Secret Service had uncovered an attempt by the German foreign minister, Alfred Zimmermann, to bribe Mexico with American territory if it entered the war on the side of Germany. Americans grew angrier.

After several more merchant ships, including three American ships, were sunk and more Americans were killed, Wilson decided on war. On April 2, 1917, the president

World War I

| Western Front |
| Map shown with pre-war national boundaries |

0 — 500 miles
0 — 500 km

ICELAND

ATLANTIC
OCEAN

NORWAY

SWEDEN

NETHERLANDS

GREAT
BRITAIN

DENMARK

RUSSIA

BELGIUM

GERMANY

LUX.

FRANCE

SWITZ.

AUSTRIA-HUNGARY

ITALY

ROMANIA

Black Sea

SPAIN

PORTUGAL

MONTENEGRO

SERBIA

BULGARIA

ALBANIA

TURKEY
(OTTOMAN EMPIRE)

GREECE

Mediterranean Sea

MOROCCO

TUNISIA

ALGERIA

Suez
Canal

(NEUTRAL AREA)

LIBYA

EGYPT

N

© Infobase Publishing

Key to Alliances in 1917

Central powers   Allied powers   Neutral nations

After World War I (1914–1918) broke out in Europe, the United States strove to remain neutral, preserving its longstanding foreign policy of isolationism. By 1917, the nation was drawn into the war to make the world "safe for democracy," in the words of President Woodrow Wilson (1913–1921). After the war, however, the nation resumed its isolationist stance, refusing to become entangled in Europe's ongoing troubles.

summoned Congress into a special session and asked for a declaration of war to make "the world safe for democracy." Congress responded on April 6, declaring war on Germany. American isolationism had ended.

See also: Axis Powers; Fourteen Points; Wilson, Woodrow.

FURTHER READING

Adams, Simon. *World War I*. New York: DK Publishing, 2007.

Brands, H.W. *Woodrow Wilson*. New York: Times Books, 2003.

World War II (1939–1945)

Worldwide conflict that started in Europe in 1939 and which the United States entered in December 1941, causing the nation to abandon once and for all its long-held foreign policy of isolationism. Throughout the 1930s, Italy, Germany, and Japan—known as the **Axis** powers—became steadily more aggressive as they demanded territory, sought power, and increased the size of their military. During the same time, however, Great Britain, France, and the United States, three of the victor nations in World War I (1914–1918), sought to maintain peace. Great Britain and France followed a policy of appeasement, while the United States, following an **isolationist** foreign policy, tried to avoid getting involved in Europe's troubles.

On September 1, 1939, Nazi Germany invaded Poland. In response, France and Great Britain declared war on Germany on September 3.

German armies soon controlled most of continental Europe, and by 1940, only Great Britain remained free from Nazi domination.

NEUTRALITY

The United States, fearful of becoming involved in another of Europe's bloody wars, committed to a policy of **neutrality,** or not taking sides. President Franklin D. Roosevelt (1933–1945) and some leaders in Congress, however, knew the nation could not afford to let Great Britain, the last remaining **democracy** in Europe, fall to the Nazis. Indeed, Roosevelt and others believed that, after conquering Britain, Nazi Germany would attack the United States as it strove to seek worldwide supremacy.

Despite the nation's officially neutral stand, the president found ways to aid Great Britain and, in early 1941, the Soviet Union, which had also been attacked by Hitler's armies. Through programs such as the Lend-Lease Act, the U.S. government sent billions of dollars worth of aid and war materials to the **Allies** who were fighting the Axis powers. At the same time, President Roosevelt began preparing the nation for war. In 1940, for example, he urged Congress to pass the first peacetime **conscription** law, drafting men into the army.

While the United States was slowly becoming involved in Europe, its diplomatic relations with Japan, an ally of Nazi Germany, steadily worsened. Determined to maintain its trade relations with China and to

World War II

Key to Areas of Control

Germany and Italy in 1937	Axis-controlled areas, mid-1942	Allied-controlled areas, mid-1942	Neutral nations

World War II (1939–1945) began in Europe when Nazi Germany invaded Poland, killing thousands of innocent civilians. The United States, following its isolationist foreign policy, refused to become involved in the conflict. However, the United States could no longer remain neutral when the Japanese Empire suddenly attacked the American naval base at Pearl Harbor, Hawaii, on December 7, 1941. In his war message to Congress, President Franklin D. Roosevelt (1933–1945) declared that day "a date that will live in infamy."

U.S. infantry wades ashore during the D-day invasion of Normandy, France, on June 6, 1944. The invasion drove German forces back from the coast, allowing the Allies to mount a coordinated offensive that ended with the defeat of Germany in May 1945.

slow or stop Japanese aggression in the Pacific region, the United States drastically cut its trade with Japan. Finally, the United States stopped all shipments to Japan of scrap iron, steel, oil, and gasoline—resources that the island nation desperately needed. Although negotiations between the two nations continued, they seemed to reach an impasse.

WAR!

At 7:55, on Sunday morning, December 7, 1941, more than 400 planes from a large Japanese fleet of six aircraft carriers struck the U.S. military base at Pearl Harbor, in Hawaii. Quickly, Japanese bombers sank five battleships and damaged three more. They damaged or destroyed many smaller ships and more than 150 American planes. The attack killed about 2,300 American sailors, marines, and soldiers and wounded 1,100 more. Later the same day, Japanese bombers destroyed most of the American planes at a base in the Philippines, then a U.S. **colony**.

On December 8, President Roosevelt addressed the U.S. Congress:

> Yesterday, December 7, 1941—a date which will live in infamy—the United States was suddenly and deliberately attacked by naval and air forces of the Empire of Japan.

Within a few hours, Congress declared war on Japan. Three days later, on December 11, Germany and Italy declared war on the United States—which in turn recognized that a state of war existed with these nations.

Allied Powers in World War II*	
Major Powers	**Minor Powers**
Great Britain	Poland
France	Belgium
Soviet Union	Denmark
United States	Norway
Australia	Luxembourg
New Zealand	Greece
Canada	Yugoslavia

*Other nations also joined the Allies but did not send troops into battle.

Thus, the isolationist foreign policy of the United States finally ended. The nation emerged from World War II a superpower and could no longer remain apart from the rest of the increasingly connected world.

See also: American First Committee; Appeasement, Policy of; Hitler, Adolf; Japan; Lend-Lease Act; World War I.

FURTHER READING

Adams, Simon. *World War II*. New York: DK Publishing, 2007.

Jenkins, Roy. *Franklin D. Roosevelt*. New York: Times Books, 2003.

Nardo, Don. *Opposing Viewpoints in World History: World War II*. Farmington Hills, Mich.: Greenhaven Press, 2005.

World Court

See League of Nations.

Young Plan

A strategy adopted in 1930 to adjust war **reparations**, or payments, owed by Germany. The heavy burden of reparations had **bankrupted** the German government and ruined the German economy. The turmoil had already inspired the Dawes Plan of 1924. Although the Dawes Plan lessened the amount of money that Germany would have to pay each year, it did not lower its total debt. Within just five years, the Dawes Plan had proven unworkable.

A NEW PLAN

The Allied Reparations Committee, representing the victorious Allies of World War I (1914–1918), convened the Second Reparations Conference to create a new and more lenient plan to replace the Dawes Plan. The committee asked an American businessman, Owen D. Young, to head this conference. As the United States did not receive direct payments from Germany, the Allied leaders thought a U.S. citizen would be the most fair in working out the renegotiation. Under the Young plan, the conference set total reparations at $26.35 billion, an amount Germany would have to pay over 58 years. Germany was to make annual payments of $473 million, but could postpone payment of two-thirds of the sum if necessary.

The Young Plan was agreed to in August 1929. It was formally adopted in January 1930, at the Hague Conference, which set up an International Bank for Settlements to handle the transfers of money. The crash of the U.S. stock market in October 1929 and the **Great Depression** that followed, plus the rapid drop in production and international trade, was causing rising unemployment in Germany and in the rest of the world. With the economy in decline, the German government was unable to collect the taxes necessary to make the scheduled payments. In 1931, the Allies agreed to a moratorium, or temporary halt, on payments from Germany. At the Lausanne Conference in 1932, the outstanding debt was reduced to less than one billion dollars. The United States also agreed to cancel all war debts owed by the Allies.

RISE OF ADOLF HITLER
The reparations had already destroyed the German economy and banking system, however, and Germany never resumed payments. (Eventually, well after the end of World War II in 1945, Germany did pay both principal and interest owed under the Young Plan.) The reparations and the harsh terms of the Treaty of Versailles became a winning campaign theme for Adolf Hitler (r. 1933–1945) and the Nazi Party, which swept into power in January 1933. Hitler repudiated the treaty after coming to power and began preparing Germany for a war of conquest and revenge in Europe.

YOUNG PLAN AND ISOLATIONISTS
The failure of the Young Plan bolstered isolationists, who used the heavy economic losses brought on by World War I to support their position. By this reasoning, the United States had been unwise to ever get involved in the war, and further entanglements with Britain, France, and Germany would only bring on more uncollectible debts and other troubles.

See also: Dawes Plan; Treaty of Versailles; World War I.

FURTHER READING
Andelman, David A. *A Shattered Peace: Versailles 1919 and the Price We Pay Today.* New York: Wiley, 2007.
Weitz, Eric D. *Weimar Germany: Promise and Tragedy.* Princeton, N.J.: Princeton University Press, 2009.

Asking Congress for War, Woodrow Wilson, 1917

Following many attempts to keep the United States out of World War I (1914–1918), President Woodrow Wilson (1913–1921) changed his stand and asked Congress for a declaration of war in April 1917. Wilson was prompted by hostile actions on the part of the Central powers and strengthening public sentiment in support of the French and British war effort.

The Germans had broken their vow to cease submarine warfare. British intelligence had also intercepted the Zimmermann telegram, a coded message to the German ambassador in Mexico urging him to foment war between Mexico and the United States. In proclaiming to Congress that "the world must be made safe for democracy," Wilson gave a rationale for abandoning the country's **neutral** stance and entering the war—a war that he had long fought to avoid.

> Armed neutrality is ineffectual enough at best; in such circumstances and in the face of such pretensions it is worse than ineffectual: it is likely only to produce what it was meant to prevent; it is practically certain to draw us into the war without either the rights or the effectiveness of belligerents. There is one choice we cannot make, we are incapable of making: we will not choose the path of submission and suffer the most sacred rights of our nation and our people to be ignored or violated. The wrongs against which we now array ourselves are no common wrongs; they cut to the very roots of human life.
>
> With a profound sense of the solemn and even tragical character of the step I am taking and of the grave responsibilities which it involves, but in unhesitating obedience to what I

(continues)

(continued)

deem my constitutional duty, I advise that the Congress declare the recent course of the Imperial German government to be in fact nothing less than war against the government and people of the United States; that it formally accept the status of belligerent which has thus been thrust upon it; and that it take immediate steps, not only to put the country in a more thorough state of defense but also to exert all its power and employ all its resources to bring the government of the German Empire to terms and end the war . . . .

Our object now, as then, is to vindicate the principles of peace and justice in the life of the world as against selfish and autocratic power and to set up among the really free and self-governed peoples of the world such a concert of purpose and of action as will henceforth ensure the observance of those principles. Neutrality is no longer feasible or desirable where the peace of the world is involved and the freedom of its peoples, and the menace to that peace and freedom lies in the existence of autocratic governments backed by organized force which is controlled wholly by their will, not by the will of their people. We have seen the last of neutrality in such circumstances. We are at the beginning of an age in which it will be insisted that the same standards of conduct and of responsibility for wrong done shall be observed among nations and their governments that are observed among the individual citizens of civilized states . . . .

The world must be made safe for democracy. Its peace must be planted upon the tested foundations of political liberty. We have no selfish ends to serve. We desire no conquest, no dominion. We seek no indemnities for ourselves, no material compensation for the sacrifices we shall freely make. We are but one of the champions of the rights of mankind. We shall be satisfied when those rights have been made as secure as the faith and the freedom of nations can make them.

Just because we fight without rancor and without selfish object, seeking nothing for ourselves but what we shall wish to share with all free peoples, we shall, I feel confident, conduct our operations as belligerents without passion and ourselves observe with proud punctilio [etiquette] the principles of right and of fair play we profess to be fighting for . . . .

It will be all the easier for us to conduct ourselves as belligerents in a high spirit of right and fairness because we act without animus, not in enmity towards a people or with the desire to bring any injury or disadvantage upon them, but only in armed opposition to an irresponsible government which has thrown aside all considerations of humanity and of right and is running amuck. We are, let me say again, the sincere friends of the German people, and shall desire nothing so much as the early reestablishment of intimate relations of mutual advantage between us—however hard it may be for them, for the time being, to believe that this is spoken from our hearts. We have borne with their present government through all these bitter months because of that friendship—exercising a patience and forbearance which would otherwise have been impossible . . . .

It is a distressing and oppressive duty, gentlemen of the Congress, which I have performed in thus addressing you. There are, it may be, many months of fiery trial and sacrifice ahead of us. It is a fearful thing to lead this great peaceful people into war, into the most terrible and disastrous of all wars, civilization itself seeming to be in the balance. But the right is more precious than peace, and we shall fight for the things which we have always carried nearest our hearts—for democracy, for the right of those who submit to authority to have a voice in their own governments, for the rights and liberties of small nations, for a universal dominion of right by such a concert of free peoples as shall bring peace and safety to all nations and make the world itself at last free. To such a task we can dedicate our lives and our fortunes, everything that we are and everything that we have, with the pride of those who know that the day has come when America is privileged to spend her blood and her might for the principles that gave her birth and happiness and the peace which she has treasured. God helping her, she can do no other.

"

 ## From the Shantung Clause, 1919

Japan had fought with the Allies against Germany in World War I (1914–1918), and even though there was little fighting in Asia, Japan was represented at the Peace Conference held in Paris in 1919. Yet, before agreeing to the Treaty of Versailles (which formally ended the war) and to join the League of Nations, Japan insisted on several concessions from Germany. These articles, known as the Shantung Clause, greatly expanded Japanese power in eastern Asia.

"

Article 156

Germany renounces, in favour of Japan, all her rights, title and privileges particularly those concerning the territory of Kiaochow, railways, mines and submarine cables which she acquired in virtue of the Treaty concluded by her with China on March 6 1898, and of all other arrangements relative to the Province of Shantung.

All German rights in the Tsingtao-Tsinanfu Railway, including its branch lines together with its subsidiary property of all kinds, stations, shops, fixed and rolling stock, mines, plant and material for the exploitation of

(continues)

(continued)

the mines, are and remain acquired by Japan, together with all rights and privileges attaching thereto.

The German State submarine cables from Tsingtao to Shanghai and from Tsingtao to Chefoo, with all the rights, privileges and properties attaching thereto, are similarly acquired by Japan, free and clear of all charges and encumbrances.

Article 157

The movable and immovable property owned by the German State in the territory of Kiaochow, as well as all the rights which Germany might claim in consequence of the works or improvements made or of the expenses incurred by her, directly or indirectly, in connection with this territory, are and remain acquired by Japan, free and clear of all charges and encumbrances.

Article 158

Germany shall hand over to Japan within three months from the coming into force of the present Treaty the archives, registers, plans, title-deeds and documents of every kind, wherever they may be, relating to the administration, whether civil, military, financial, judicial or other, of the territory of Kiaochow.

Within the same period Germany shall give particulars to Japan of all treaties, arrangements or agreements relating to the rights, title or privileges referred to in the two preceding Articles.

"

❗ *From the Peace for Our Time speech, Prime Minister Neville Chamberlain, 1938*

In 1938, the leaders of the Soviet Union, Germany, Britain, France, and Italy met in Munich, Germany, to discuss Germany's attempt to annex the Sudetenland, a part of Czechoslovakia with a large ethnic German population. This conference came to be known as the Munich Conference. While there, the **Allies** agreed to the demands of Germany's Nazi dictator, Adolf Hitler (r. 1933–1945).

After returning from the Munich Conference, British prime minister Neville Chamberlain (r. 1937–1940), standing in front of the prime minister's residence in London, gave the following speech. The speech is striking because the countries' agreement to allow Germany's takeover of the lands was followed quickly by invasions throughout Europe. The policy to which the Allies agreed in Munich became known as appeasement.

" We, the German Fuhrer and Chancellor, and the British Prime Minister, have had a further meeting today and are agreed in recognizing that the question of Anglo-German relations is of the first importance for our two countries and for Europe.

We regard the agreement signed last night and the Anglo-German Naval Agreement as symbolic of the desire of our two peoples never to go to war with one another again.

We are resolved that the method of consultation shall be the method adopted to deal with any other questions that may concern our two countries, and we are determined to continue our efforts to remove possible sources of difference, and thus to contribute to assure the peace of Europe.

My good friends, for the second time in our history, a British Prime Minister has returned from Germany bringing peace with honor. I believe it is "peace for our time." Go home and get a nice quiet sleep. "

Speaking Against Involvement, Charles A. Lindbergh, September 11, 1941

Charles A. Lindbergh had won international renown for his courageous solo flight from New York to Paris in 1927. He had also gained the public's sympathy and support through the ordeal of his infant son's kidnapping and murder, which took place in 1932. After the outbreak of World War II (1939–1945), he became an outspoken leader of the America First Committee. This organization strongly opposed U.S. involvement in Europe's troubles and wars. Lindbergh was thought to be **anti-Semitic**, and some Americans, including President Franklin D. Roosevelt (1933–1945), believed he was even a Nazi sympathizer, reasons said to contribute to his **isolationist** thinking. In this excerpt, Lindbergh identifies the groups that he considers to be working to engage the nation in World War II (1939–1945).

" It is now two years since this latest European war began. From that day in September, 1939, until the present moment, there has been an over-increasing effort to force the United States into the conflict.

That effort has been carried on by foreign interests, and by a small minority of our own people; but it has been so successful that, today, our country stands on the verge of war.

At this time, as the war is about to enter its third winter, it seems appropriate to review the circumstances that have led us to our present position. Why are we on the verge of war? Was it necessary for us to become so deeply involved? Who is responsible for changing our national policy from one of neutrality and independence to one of entanglement in European affairs?

Personally, I believe there is no better argument against our intervention than a study of the causes and developments of the present war. I have often said that if the true facts and issues were placed before the American people, there would be no danger of our involvement.

Here, I would like to point out to you a fundamental difference between the groups who advocate foreign war, and those who believe in an independent destiny for America.

If you will look back over the record, you will find that those of us who oppose intervention have constantly tried to clarify facts and issues; while the interventionists have tried to hide facts and confuse issues.

We ask you to read what we said last month, last year, and even before the war began. Our record is open and clear, and we are proud of it.

We have not led you on by subterfuge and propaganda. We have not resorted to steps short of anything, in order to take the American people where they did not want to go.

What we said before the elections, we say [illegible] and again, and again today. And we will not tell you tomorrow that it was just campaign oratory. Have you ever heard an interventionist, or a British agent, or a member of the administration in Washington ask you to go back and study a record of what they have said since the war started? Are their self-styled defenders of democracy willing to put the issue of war to a vote of our people? Do you find these crusaders for foreign freedom of speech, or the removal of censorship here in our own country?

The subterfuge and propaganda that exists in our country is obvious on every side. Tonight, I shall try to pierce through a portion of it, to the naked facts which lie beneath.

When this war started in Europe, it was clear that the American people were solidly opposed to entering it. Why shouldn't we be? We had the best defensive position in the world; we had a tradition of independence from Europe; and the one time we did take part in a European war left European problems unsolved, and debts to America unpaid.

National polls showed that when England and France declared war on Germany, in 1939, less than 10 percent of our population favored a similar course for America. But there were various groups of people, here and abroad, whose interests and beliefs necessitated the involvement of the United States in the war. I shall point out some of these groups tonight, and outline their methods of procedure. In doing this, I must speak with the utmost frankness, for in order to counteract their efforts, we must know exactly who they are.

The three most important groups who have been pressing this country toward war are the British, the Jewish and the Roosevelt administration.

Behind these groups, but of lesser importance, are a number of capitalists, Anglophiles, and intellectuals who believe that the future of mankind depends upon the domination of the British empire. Add to these the Communistic groups who were opposed to intervention until a few weeks ago, and I believe I have named the major war agitators in this country. . . . ”

From the Lend-Lease Act, 1941

At the beginning of World War II (1939–1945), the United States maintained a policy of **neutrality**. By early 1941, however, Nazi German armies had conquered much of continental Europe, leaving only Great Britain to fight Hitler's forces. President Franklin D. Roosevelt (1933–1945) proposed the Lend-Lease Act to help Britain obtain arms and munitions, but at the same time maintain America's official neutrality. Congress passed the Lend-Lease Act on March 11, 1941.

AN ACT

Further to promote the defense of the United States, and for other purposes.

Be it enacted by the Senate and House of Representatives of the United States of America in Congress assembled, That this Act may be cited as "An Act to Promote the Defense of the United States". . . .

SEC. 3. (a) Notwithstanding the provisions of any other law, the President may, from time to time, when he deems it in the interest of national defense, authorize the Secretary Of War, the Secretary of the Navy, or the head of any other department or agency of the Government—

(1) To manufacture in arsenals, factories, and shipyards under

(continues)

(continued)

their jurisdiction, or otherwise procure, to the extent to which funds are made available therefor, or contracts are authorized from time to time by the Congress, or both, any defense article for the government of any country whose defense the President deems vital to the defense of the United States.

(2) To sell, transfer title to, exchange, lease, lend, or otherwise dispose of, to any such government any defense article, but no defense article not manufactured or procured under paragraph (1) shall in any way be disposed of under this paragraph, except after consultation with the Chief of Staff of the Army or the Chief of Naval Operations of the Navy, or both. The value of defense articles disposed of in any way under authority of this paragraph, and procured from funds heretofore appropriated, shall not exceed $1,300,000,000. The value of such defense articles shall be determined by the head of the department or agency concerned or such other department, agency or officer as shall be designated in the manner provided in the rules and regulations issued hereunder. Defense articles procured from funds hereafter appropriated to any department or agency of the Government, other than from funds authorized to be appropriated under this Act, shall not be disposed of in any way under

authority of this paragraph except to the extent hereafter authorized by the Congress in the Acts appropriating such funds or otherwise.

(3) To test, inspect, prove, repair, outfit, recondition, or otherwise to place in good working order, to the extent to which funds are made available therefor, or contracts are authorized from time to time by the Congress, or both, any defense article for any such government, or to procure any or all such services by private contract.

(4) To communicate to any such government any defense information pertaining to any defense article furnished to such government under paragraph (2) of this subsection.

(5) To release for export any defense article disposed of in any way under this subsection to any such government.

(b) The terms and conditions upon which any such foreign government receives any aid authorized under subsection (a) shall be those which the President deems satisfactory, and the benefit to the United States may be payment or repayment in kind or property, or any other direct or indi-rect benefit which the President deems satisfactory.

(c) After June 30, 1943, or after the passage of a concurrent resolution by the two Houses before June 30, 1943, which declares that the powers con-ferred by or pursuant to subsection (a) are no longer necessary to pro-mote the defense of the United

States, neither the President nor the head of any department or agency shall exercise any of the powers conferred by or pursuant to subsection (a) except that until July 1, 1946, any of such powers may be exercised to the extent necessary to carry out a contract or agreement with such a foreign government made before July 1,1943, or before the passage of such concurrent resolution, whichever is the earlier.

(d) Nothing in this Act shall be construed to authorize or to permit the authorization of convoying vessels by naval vessels of the United States.

(e) Nothing in this Act shall be construed to authorize or to permit the authorization of the entry of any American vessel into a combat area in violation of section 3 of the neutrality Act of 1939.

SEC. 4. All contracts or agreements made for the disposition of any defense article or defense information pursuant to section 3 shall contain a clause by which the foreign government undertakes that it will not, without the consent of the President, transfer title to or possession of such defense article or defense information by gift, sale, or otherwise, or permit its use by anyone not an officer, employee, or agent of such foreign government.

SEC. 5. (a) The Secretary of War, the Secretary of the Navy, or the head of any other department or agency of the Government involved shall when any such defense article

or defense information is exported, immediately inform the department or agency designated by the President to administer section 6 of the Act of July 2, 1940 (54 Stat. 714) of the quantities, character, value, terms of disposition and destination of the article and information so exported.

(b) The President from time to time, but not less frequently than once every ninety days, shall transmit to the Congress a report of operations under this Act except such information as he deems incompatible with the public interest to disclose. Reports provided for under this subsection shall be transmitted to the Secretary of the Senate or the Clerk of the House of Representatives, as the case may be, if the Senate or the House of Representatives, as the case may be, is not in session.

SEC. 6. (a) There is hereby authorized to be appropriated from time to time, out of any money in the Treasury not otherwise appropriated, such amounts as may be necessary to carry out the provisions and accomplish the purposes of this Act.

(b) All money and all property which is converted into money received under section 3 from any government shall, with the approval of the Director of the Budget, revert to the respective appropriation or appropriations out of which funds were expended with respect to the defense article or defense information for which such consideration is received, and shall be available for

(continues)

(continued)

expenditure for the purpose for which such expended funds were appropriated by law, during the fiscal year in which such funds are received and the ensuing fiscal year; but in no event shall any funds so received be available for expenditure after June 30, 1946.

SEC. 7. The Secretary of War, the Secretary of the Navy, and the head of the department or agency shall in all contracts or agreements for the disposition of any defense article or defense information fully protect the rights of all citizens of the United States who have patent rights in and to any such article or information which is hereby authorized to be disposed of and the payments collected for royalties on such patents shall be paid to the owners and holders of such patents.

SEC. 8. The Secretaries of War and of the Navy are hereby authorized to purchase or otherwise acquire arms, ammunition, and implements of war produced within the jurisdiction of any country to which section 3 is applicable, whenever the President deems such purchase or acquisition to be necessary in the interests of the defense of the United States.

SEC. 9. The President may, from time to time, promulgate such rules and regulations as may be necessary and proper to carry out any of the provisions of this Act; and he may exercise any power or authority conferred on him by this Act through such department, agency, or officer as be shall direct.

SEC. 10. Nothing in this Act shall be construed to change existing law relating to the use of the land and naval forces of the United States, except insofar as such use relates to the manufacture, procurement, and repair of defense articles, the communication of information and other noncombatant purposes enumerated in this Act.

SEC 11. If any provision of this Act or the application of such provision to any circumstance shall be held invalid, the validity of the remainder of the Act and the applicability of such provision to other circumstances shall not be affected thereby. **"**

abdication The act of surrendering a title or authority.

Allies The group of nations who fought the Central Powers of Germany and Austria-Hungary in World War I; also, the nations who fought the Axis in World War II.

amendment A change to a document or process.

anarchists Those who oppose any form of law and government.

annexation The occupation and permanent control of a territory.

anti-Semitism Discrimination against or the expression of prejudice or hostility toward Jews.

armistice A truce to halt fighting while the opposing sides negotiate a permanent peace.

Axis (Axis powers) The losing side in World War II.

bankrupt Unable to pay off debts or other liabilities.

bilateral Two-sided, as in a truce or formal agreement.

bipartisan An agreement between two sides or political parties.

blockade The act of halting a nation's trade by preventing ships or other means of transport from reaching it.

Bolshevik A member of the radical wing of the Russian Socialist Party, which carried out the 1917 Russian Revolution.

boycott To refuse to buy goods to force a change in policy.

capitalism An economic system in which wealth and the means of production are owned by private individuals.

capitalist One who supports an economic system based on private property and the profit motive.

census A regular count of a nation's population.

civil rights era Beginning in the 1950s, the time when African Americans sought equal rights.

coalition An alliance of two or more factions to achieve a certain goal, such as winning a war or an election.

colony A settlement established in a new land controlled by a parent country.

Communist Adhering to an economic system (**communism**) in which the state, under the control of a single political party, owns property and the means of production.

conscription Forced participation in the armed forces.

conservative Individual opposed to rapid change in society.

democracy A political system in which the people have the right to express their views and vote for representatives.

depression A period of deep economic slowdown characterized by high unemployment, business closures, and an unwillingness of banks to issue credit.

disarmament The policy of reducing or eliminating the military power of a nation or group of nations.

dissent Disagreement with policies or principles.

economic sanctions Restrictions on trade meant to force a nation to take a specific action.

emancipation Freedom from bondage.

embargo A ban on the trade of certain goods.

Fascist Member of a strongly nationalistic political party or movement that favors centralized control of laws, society, and the economy.

genocide Systematic murder of a national, racial, political or cultural group. The term was coined after World War II to describe the murder of millions of Jews by the Germans during the Holocaust.

ghetto An area, usually restricted by discrimination or economic pressure, where people of the same race, religion, or ethnic group live.

Great Depression Worldwide economic collapse in the 1930s.

gross national product (GNP) A number representing the total financial output of a country in a given year; the number includes the value of all goods and services produced within a country.

hijacked The act of illegally taking over an aircraft, ship, or vehicle.

Holocaust The systematic extermination of more than 6 million European Jews by Nazi Germany during the course of World War II (1939–1945).

hyperinflation A collapse in the value of money causing a sharp rise in prices.

immigrant Someone who moves from their home country to settle in a different country.

immigration The movement of people into a new country.

imperialism A policy of imposing political and economic control on colonies.

impressed To be taken prisoner and forced into military service.

inauguration The ceremony that marks the formal beginning of a term of service, such as that of a president.

incumbent The holder of an office.

industrialization The process of moving from an agriculturally based society to one based on business and manufacturing.

insurgents Those who rebel against an established political authority.

internationalists Those who favor involvement in world affairs.

interventionist One who advocates involvement in foreign conflict.

Irreconcilables Term for the group of senators who opposed ratification of the Treaty of Versailles in any form.

isolationist(s) Opposing (or those who oppose) involvement in foreign affairs.

laissez-faire A term that describes a government policy of little involvement in the economy.

lynching An act of mob violence to punish a person for a supposed crime outside of the justice system.

mandate Governance of a foreign territory through the terms of a treaty.

manifest destiny Term used to describe the belief that the United States was destined to expand across North America.

manifesto A public declaration of principles or policies, especially of a political nature.

Marxists Followers of the ideas of Karl Marx, a German economist who foresaw conflict among different classes and revolution on the part of the world's industrial workers.

monarch A person, such as a king or queen, who rules over a kingdom or empire.

monarchists Those who favor a monarchy.

multilateral Agreed upon by several parties or nations.

nationalism A view that supports the culture, society, and political system, of one's own country over those of foreign nations.

nativists Those who strongly favor the culture of their own country and who see outside influences as a threat.

neutral Not taking sides, especially in war.

New Deal A series of laws passed during the administration of President Franklin D. Roosevelt (1933–1945), designed to lessen the effects of the Great Depression of the 1930s.

nonintervention The policy of avoiding conflict in foreign nations.

offensive A coordinated military assault meant to seize territory and place the enemy on the defensive.

pacifist One who is opposed to war or violence as a means of settling disputes.

partisans Those fighting for a cause outside of national armed forces.

prejudice A negative view of an individual or group of individuals.

Progressive Member of an early twentieth century political movement who sought better working conditions in factories and protection of the poor.

propaganda Information, ideas, or rumors deliberately spread to help or harm a person, group, or nation.

protectionism A policy of supporting an economy by preventing foreign imports and competition.

protectorate A territory under the occupation of another nation.

provisional Temporary.

Quakers Also called the Society of Friends, a Christian religious sect that does not have a clergy.

quota A prescribed number or quantity.

ransom A sum of money demanded for the release of people who have been kidnapped.

ratification The passage of a treaty or constitutional change.

Reconstruction The period immediately after the Civil War (1861–1865) during which social structures and the economy of the South were rebuilt; marked by the presence of federal troops in the former Confederate states until 1877.

reparations Payment for war damages.

republican Relating to a republic, a form of government in which the people rule.

sanctions Penalties imposed to bring about a change in policy.

socialism An economic system that favors public ownership of the means of production and property.

Socialist An advocate of governmental ownership of resources and the means of production.

sovereignty Self-rule by a society.

tariff A tax on imported goods.

totalitarian state Of or relating to a government which exercises absolute control over all aspects of life.

trench warfare From 1917, fighting in which opposing forces attack each other from a relatively permanent system of trenches protected by barbed wire.

tyranny A government characterized by the rule of an individual or faction.

unilateral Action taken by one party or side, with or without the consent of others.

veto Rejection of a law or agreement by a head of state.

Selected Bibliography

1918: A Flawed Victory. The Grolier Library of World War I. Danbury, Conn.: Grolier Educational, 1997.

Adams, Simon. *World War II.* DK Eyewitness Books. New York: DK Children, 2007.

Ambrosius, Lloyd. *Wilsonian Statecraft: The Theory and Practice of Liberal Internationalism During World War I.* Wilmington, Dela.: SR Books, 2001.

Andelman, David A. *A Shattered Peace: Versailles 1919 and the Price We Pay Today.* New York: Wiley, 2007.

Ashby, Leroy. *The Spearless Leader: Senator Borah & the Progressive Movement in the 1920s.* Champaign: University of Illinois Press, 1972.

BBC Online: "World War II." Available online. URL: http://www.bbc.co.uk/history/worldwars/wwtwo/

Beach, Edward L. *Scapegoats: A Defense of Kimmel and Short at Pearl Harbor.* Annapolis, Md.: Naval Institute Press, 1995.

Berg, A. Scott. *Lindbergh.* New York: Putnam, 1998.

Bix, Herbert. *Hirohito and the Making of Modern Japan.* New York: Harper Perennial, 2001.

Bloch, Marc. *Strange Defeat.* New York: W.W. Norton, 2001.

Bosworth, R.J.B. *Mussolini's Italy: Life Under the Fascist Dictatorship, 1915–1945.* New York: Penguin Books, 2007.

Chambers, John W., II, ed. *The Eagle and the Dove: The American Peace Movement and United States Foreign Policy, 1900–1922.* Syracuse, N.Y.: Syracuse University Press, 1992.

Chatfield, Charles. *For Peace and Justice: Pacifism in America, 1914–1941.* Knoxville: University of Tennessee Press, 1971.

Churchill, Winston. *The Gathering Storm.* Boston: Mariner Books, 1986.

Coetzee, Frans, and Marilyn Shevin-Coetzee. *World War I: A History in Documents.* New York: Oxford University Press, 2002.

Coolidge, Calvin, and Peter Hannaford. *The Quotable Calvin Coolidge: Sensible Words for a New Century.* Bennington, Vt.: Images from the Past, 2001.

Costello, John. *Days of Infamy: MacArthur, Roosevelt, Churchill—The Shocking Truth Revealed.* New York: Pocket Books, 1994.

Craats, Rennay. *History of the 1920s.* New York: Weigl Publishers, 2001.

Daniels, Roger. *Coming to America: A History of Immigration and Ethnicity in American Life.* Second edition. New York: Harper Perennial, 2002.

Dinardo, R.L. *Germany and the Axis Powers: From Coalition to Collapse.* Lawrence: University Press of Kansas, 2005.

Dinnerstein, Leonard. *Ethnic Americans: A History of Immigration.* New York: Columbia University Press, 1999.

Doenecke, Justus D. *In Danger Undaunted: The Anti-Interventionist Movement of 1940–1941 as Revealed in the Papers of the America First Committee.* Stanford, Calif.: Hoover Institution, 1990.

——. *Storm on the Horizon: The Challenge to American Intervention, 1939–1941.* Oxford, UK: Oxford University Press, 2000.

Eksteins, Modris. *Rites of Spring: The Great War and the Birth of the Modern Age.* New York: Doubleday, 1990.

Esposito, John. *The Legacy of Woodrow Wilson: American War Aims in World War I.* Westport, Conn.: Praeger Publishers, 1996.

Fromkin, David. *Europe's Last Summer: Who Started the Great War in 1914?* New York: Vintage, 2005.

Fuchs, Thomas. *A Concise Biography of Adolf Hitler*. New York: Berkley Books, 2000.

Fussell, Paul. *Wartime: Understanding and Behavior in the Second World War*. New York: Oxford University Press, 1989.

Gilbert, Martin. *The First World War: A Complete History*. New York: Henry Holt, 1994.

Goldstein, Erik. *The First World War Peace Settlements, 1919–1925*. Upper Saddle River, N.J.: Longman, 2002.

Graham, Otis. *Unguarded Gates: A History of America's Immigration Crisis*. Lanham, Md.: Rowman & Littlefield, 2006.

Grenville, J.A.S. *A History of the World in the Twentieth Century*. Cambridge, Mass.: Belknap Press of Harvard University Press, 1994.

Henig, Ruth. *Versailles and After: 1919–1933*. New York: Routledge, 1995.

Henshall, Kenneth G. *A History of Japan, Second Edition: From Stone Age to Superpower*. London: Palgrave Macmillan, 2004.

Hibbert, Christopher. *Mussolini: The Rise and Fall of Il Duce*. New York: Palgrave Macmillan, 2008.

History.com. "Isolationism." Available online. URL: http://www.history.com/encyclopedia.do?articleId=212955

History Learning Site. "Treaty of Versailles." Available online. URL: http://www.historylearningsite.co.uk/treaty_of_versailles.htm

Hixson, Walter L. *Charles A. Lindbergh: Lone Eagle*. Upper Saddle River, N.J.: Longman, 2006.

HyperWar: A Hypertext History of the Second World War. Available online. URL: http://www.ibiblio.org/hyperwar/

Isserman, Maurice. *World War II*. America at War series. New York: Facts On File, 1991.

Kauffman, Bill. *America First! Its History, Culture, and Politics*. Amherst, N.Y.: Prometheus Books, 1995.

Keegan, John. *An Illustrated History of the First World War*. New York: Alfred A. Knopf, 2001.

———. *The First World War*. New York: Vintage, 2000.

Kennedy, David M. *Over Here: The First World War and American Society*. Oxford: Oxford University Press, 1980.

Kent, Bruce. *The Spoils of War: The Politics, Economics, and Diplomacy of Reparations, 1918–1932*. New York: Oxford University Press, 1992.

Kimball, Husband E. *Admiral Kimmel's Story*. Chicago: Henry Regnery Co., 1995.

Knock, Thomas J. *To End All Wars: Woodrow Wilson and the Quest for a New World Order*. New York: Oxford University Press, 1992.

Layton, Edward T. *"And I Was There": Pearl Harbor and Midway—Breaking the Secrets*. New York: William Morrow and Co., 1985.

Lindbergh, Charles A. *The Spirit of St. Louis*. New York: Scribner, 2003.

MacLean, Nancy K. *Behind the Mask of Chivalry: The Making of the Second Ku Klux Klan*. New York: Oxford University Press, 1995.

Marks, Frederick W., III. *Wind over Sand: The Diplomacy of Franklin Roosevelt*. Athens: University of Georgia Press, 1988.

Marr, Andrew. *A History of Modern Britain*. London: Macmillan UK, 2008.

Marshall, Jonathan. *To Have and Have Not: Southeast Asian Raw Materials and the Origins of the Pacific War*. Berkeley: University of California Press, 1995.

Martel, Gordon. *Origins of the First World War*. Revised Third Edition. Upper Saddle River, N.J.: Longman, 2008.

McCartney, Laton. *The Teapot Dome Scandal: How Big Oil Bought the Harding White House and Tried to Steal the Country*. New York: Random House Trade Paperback, 2009.

McDonough, Frank. *Hitler, Chamberlain, and Appeasement*. New York: Cambridge University Press, 2002.

Murphy, Donald. *America's Entry into World War I.* Farmington Hills, Mich.: Greenhaven Press, 2004.

Nardo, Don, ed. *World War II.* Opposing Viewpoints in World History series. Farmington Hills, Mich.: Greenhaven Press, 2005.

Neville, Peter. *Hitler and Appeasement: The British Attempt to Prevent the Second World War.* London and New York: Hambledon & Continuum, 2007.

Newton, Michael. *The Ku Klux Klan: History, Organization, Language, Influence, and Activities of America's Most Notorious Secret Society.* Jefferson, N.C.: McFarland and Company, 2006.

Ninkovich, Frank. *The Wilsonian Century: U.S. Foreign Policy Since 1900.* Chicago and London: University of Chicago Press, 1999.

Nisbet, Robert. *Roosevelt and Stalin: The Failed Courtship.* Washington, D.C.: Regnery Gateway, 1988.

Popkin, Jeremy D. *A History of Modern France.* Third Edition. Englewood Cliffs, N.J.: Prentice-Hall, 2005.

Powaski, Ronald E. *Toward an Entangling Alliance: American Isolationism, Internationalism and Europe, 1901–1950.* New York: Greenwood Press, 1991.

Rogers, James T. *Woodrow Wilson, Visionary for Peace.* Makers of America. New York: Facts On File, 1997.

Rossina, Daniela, ed. *From Theodore Roosevelt to FDR: Internationalism and Isolationism in American Foreign Policy.* Staffordshire, England: Ryburn, 1995.

Rusbridger, James, and Eric Nave. *Betrayal at Pearl Harbor: How Churchill Lured Roosevelt into World War II.* New York: Summit Books, 1991.

Schaffer, Ronald. *America in the Great War: The Rise of the War Welfare State.* Oxford: Oxford University Press, 1991.

Schogan, Ronald. *Hard Bargain: How FDR Twisted Churchill's Arm, Evaded the Law and Changed the Role of the American Presidency.* New York: Scribner, 1995.

Self, Robert C. *Neville Chamberlain: A Biography.* Farnham, England: Ashgate Publishing, 2007.

Shirer, William. *The Collapse of the Third Republic.* New York: Da Capo Press, 1994.

Smith, Page. *America Enters the World.* New York: McGraw-Hill, 1985.

Sobel, Richard. *Coolidge.* Washington, D.C.: Regnery Publishing, 2000.

Spartacus Educational. "Second World War." Available online. URL: http://www.spartacus.schoolnet.co.uk/2WW.htm

Stenehjem, Michele Flynn. *An American First: John T. Flynn and the America First Committee.* New Rochelle, N.Y.: Arlington House, Publishers, 1976.

Suvorov, Viktor. *Icebreaker: Who Started the Second World War?* London: Hamish Hamilton, 1990.

Swain, Carol M., ed. *Debating Immigration.* New York: Cambridge University Press, 2007.

Thompson, Robert Smith. *A Time for War: Franklin D. Roosevelt and the Path to Pearl Harbor.* New York: Prentice Hall Press, 1991.

U-S-History.com.: "Isolationism." Available online. URL: http://www.u-s-history.com/pages/h1601.html

U.S. Department of State. "Diplomacy in Action: Isolationism in the 1930s." Available online. URL: http://www.state.gov/r/pa/ho/time/wwii/102129.htm

Wade, Wyn Craig. *The Fiery Cross: The Ku Klux Klan in America.* New York: Oxford University Press, 1998.

Ward, Geoffrey C. *The War: An Intimate History, 1941–1945.* New York: Alfred A. Knopf, 2007.

Weitz, Eric D. *Weimar Germany: Promise and Tragedy.* Princeton, N.J.: Princeton University Press, 2009.

Winter, Jay, and Blaine Baggett. *The First World War and the Shaping of the Twentieth Century.* New York: Penguin Books, 1996.

Index

Page numbers in **boldface** indicate topics covered in depth in the **A** to **Z** section of the book.

A

Acerbo Law, 57
Adams, John, 2
Adams, John Quincy, 55
Afghanistan, 8–9
African Americans, 42–43
airmail, 49–50
al Qaeda, 8–9, 65
Albania, 15, 58
Allied Powers. *see* World War I; World War II
America First Committee (AFC), **11–13**, 40, 50, 61, 67
Anarchist Exclusion Act, 62
Anti-Comintern Pact, 15
Anti-Defamation League (ADL), 43
anti-Semitism, 12, 35–36, 42, 50–51
appeasement, policy of, **13–14**, 31–32, 33
atomic bombs, 16
Australia, 41
Austria, 12, 14, 20, 31, 37, 81
Austria-Hungary. *see* Central Powers; World War I
Axis powers, **14–16**. *see also* World War II

B

Belgium, 41
Birth of a Nation (film), 42
Blaine, John, 41
Bolsheviks, 39, 62, 69, 71, 74–76
Borah, William E., 3, **16–18**, 29–30, 44, 72, 73
Brewster, Kingman, 11
Briand, Aristide, 40
Bulgaria, 18–20
Bush, George H. W., 8
Butler, Nicholas Murray, 40

C

Canada, 41
Central Powers, **18–20**, 86
Chamberlain, Neville, 13–14, 33
Clayton Antitrust Act, 88
Clemenceau, Georges, 31
Clinton, Bill, 8
Cold War, 7–8, 48
colonization, 54
Communism, 7–8, 12, 48, 59, 68, 74–75. *see also* Red Scare
Coolidge, Calvin, 5, **20–22**, 40–41, 71–72
Czechoslovakia, 14, 41

D

Dawes, Charles, 22–23, 84
Dawes Plan, **22–23**, 84–85, 97
Debs, Eugene V., 69
Democratic Party, **23–25**
Detzer, Dorothy, 60–61
disarmament, 13, 27, 45

E

Emergency Quota Act, **25–26**
Espionage Act, 62, 69
Ethiopia, 58

F

Fascism, 55–57
Federal Reserve System, 88
Federal Trade Commission (FTC), 88
Ferdinand, Franz, 20, 90
Fordney-McCumber tariff, 71, 76
Forrest, Nathan Bedford, 42
Fourteen Points, **26–30**, 44, 73, 79–80, 89

France
about, **30–32**
and Kellogg-Briand Pact, 40–41
and Russian Civil War, 75
and Treaty of Versailles, 80
in World War I, 19–20, 30–31, 90–92
in World War II, 32, 38
Frank, Leo, 42

G

Germany. *see also* World War II
as Axis power, 15–16
as Central power, 18–20
and Kellogg-Briand Pact, 41
and Russia, 75
war reparations of, 22–23, 84
and World War I, 90–94
Grant, Madison, 59
Great Britain, 5, 19–20, **32–34**, 54–55, 75, 79, 90–92
Great Depression, 23, 39, 64, 72, 76–77, 85

H

Harding, Warren G., 21, **34–35**, 53, 71
Hawley, Willis, 76
Hitler, Adolf
about, 5–6, **33–38**
and appeasement, 13–14
and Axis powers, 15–16
and Charles Lindbergh, 51
rise of, 23, 31, 44, 80, 81–82, 84, 98
William Borah on, 18
Hoover, Herbert, 72, 77
Hoover, J. Edgar, 62–63, 70

I

immigration, 4, 21–22, 25–26, 42–43, 58–60, 71
Immigration Act of 1917, 26
Immigration Act of 1924, 1, 21–22, 26. *see also* National Origins Act
India, 27, 41
Industrial Workers of the World (IWW), 69–70
Ireland, 27, 41
Islam, 9–10
Italy
    as Axis power, 14–16, 37
    under Benito Mussolini, 55–58
    as Central power, 19–20
    and Kellogg-Briand Pact, 41
    and Treaty of Versailles, 80
    in World War I, 90–91

J

Japan. *see also* Pearl Harbor; World War II
    about, **38–40**
    as Axis power, 15–16
    invasion of China by, 13
    and Kellogg-Briand Pact, 41
    in World War I, 91
Jefferson, Thomas, 2
Jews. *see* anti-Semitism
Johnson, Albert, 59
Johnson, Paul, 4
Johnson-Reed Act. *see* Immigration Act of 1924; National Origins Act

K

Kanji, Ishiwara, 39
Kellogg, Frank, 22, 40
Kellogg-Briand Pact, 22, **40–42**, 72
Kimmel, Husband, 67–68
Knox, Frank, 67
Korea, 7
Ku Klux Klan (KKK), 4, 25–26, **42–43**

L

La Follette, Robert, 11, 72
laissez-faire, 21
League of Nations. *see also* Borah, William E.; Lodge, Henry Cabot; Treaty of Versailles
    about, 3, **43–46**
    and Calvin Coolidge, 22
    formation of, 13, 23–24, 27–29, 39, 81, 82–83
    and Fourteen Points, 27
    and Germany, 14
    opposition to, 73–74
    support for, 31
    and Warren Harding, 34
Lend-Lease program, 7, 12, 33, **46–48**, 72, 94
Lenin, Vladimir I., 62, 69, 75
Lindbergh, Charles A., 11–12, **48–51**, 67
Lodge, Henry Cabot
    about, **51–53**
    and Fourteen Points, 29–30
    opposition to League of Nations, 3, 44, 72, 73–74, 81, 89
Lusitania (ship), 3, 88, 89, 92
Luther, Martin, 35

M

Maginot Line, 31–32
manifest destiny, 2, 53
Marshall Plan, 7, 68
McCormick, Robert, 11
Mein Kampf (Hitler), 37, 81
Monroe, James, 53–55
Monroe Doctrine, 2, **53–55**
Munich Agreement, 14, 32, 33, 37–38
munitions companies, 60–61
Mussolini, Benito, 5–6, 14–15, 16, **55–58**

N

National Origins Act, **58–60**. *see also* Immigration Act of 1924
Naval Expansion Act, 65
Nazi Party, 35–37

neutrality, 3, 46, 61, 91, 94–95
Neutrality Acts, 5–6, 24, 47, 72, 90
New Deal, 18, 24, 60, 65
New Freedom, 87–88
New Zealand, 41
Norris, George, 60–61
Nye, Gerald P., 11, **60–61**, 72

O

O'Sullivan, John, 2
Ottoman Empire, 18–20

P

Pact of Steel, 58
Palmer, A. Mitchell, 61–63, 70, 71
Palmer raids, **61–63**
Pearl Harbor, 7, 15, 33, 38, **63–69**, 96
Permanent Court of International Justice (PCIJ), 46
Persian Gulf War, 8
Poland, 38, 41, 94
Post, Louis, 63
Princep, Gavrilo, 91
protectionism, 76

R

racism, 25, 35–36, 42–43
Reciprocal Agreements Act, 77
Red Scare, 26, 30, 61–63, **69–71**. *see also* Communism
Reed, David, 59
Republican Party, **71–72**
reservationists, 29, **73–74**
The Rising Tide of Color against White World Supremacy (Stoddard), 59
Roberts, Owen, 68
Roberts Commission, 68
Roosevelt, Franklin D.
    and Charles Lindbergh, 50–51
    criticism against, 11–12
    and Democratic Party, 24–25
    and Henry Lodge, 51–52
    and Neutrality Acts, 47

and the New Deal, 18
and Smoot-Hawley tariff,
    77
and World War II, 5–7, 15,
    33, 64–68, 97
Round Robin Petition, 44
Russia. *see also* Soviet Union
and Red Scare, 69–70
Revolution/Civil War in,
    39, 62, 64, 74–76
and U.S. expansion, 2
in World War I, 90–91
Russian Revolution and Civil
    War, 39, 62, 64, **74–76**

S

Sedition Act, 62, 69
September 11 attacks, 8–9,
    65
Serbia, 90–91
Shantung Clause. *see* Treaty
    of Versailles
Short, Walter, 67–68
Shotwell, James T., 40
Simmons, William Joseph,
    42
Smoot, Reed, 76
Smoot-Hawley Tariff, **76–77**
South Africa, 41
Soviet Union. *see also* Russia
and Anti-Comintern Pact,
    15
collapse of, 8, 9
establishment of, 74
and Lend-Lease Act, 33, 48,
    94
and World War II, 7
Stephenson, Grand Dragon
    D. C., 43
Stimson, Henry, 72
Stimson Doctrine, 72
Stoddard, Lothrop, 59
Stuart, R. Douglas, 11

T

Taft, William Howard, 87
terrorism, 8–10, 65
Thomas, Norman, **77–78**
Treaty of Brest-Litovsk,
    75
Treaty of Versailles. *see also*
    League of Nations
about, 3–4, **78–83**
and Japan, 39
opposition to, 73–74,
    89–90
renunciation of, 14–15
terms of, 22, 27–29, 80–
    81, 89
violations of, 31, 37
Tripartite Pact, 15
Triple Alliance, 19–20, 90
Triple Entente, 19–20, 38, 90
Trotsky, Leon, 75

U

Underwood-Simmons Tariff,
    88
United Kingdom, 41
United Nations, 45, 46

V

Vietnam War, 7–8, 48

W

War of 1812, 2
war reparations, 4, **84–85**.
    see also Dawes Plan;
    Young Plan
Washington, George, 1, 84,
    85–86
Washington's Farewell
    Address, 1, 84, **85–
    86**
Wilhelm II, 36, 80

Wilson, Woodrow
about, 34, **86–90**
and Henry Lodge, 52
and immigration, 26
and League of Nations,
    23–24, 44–45, 73–74
and Red Scare, 62–63, 71
and Russian Civil War, 75
and Treaty of Versailles,
    79–80, 81
and World War I, 3, 91–94
Wood, Robert, 11
World War I. *see also* Treaty
    of Versailles
about, 3, **90–94**
Central Powers in, 18–20
France in, 19–20, 30–31,
    90–92
Great Britain in, 32
isolationism after, 31
and Thomas Norman, 78
World War II. *see also* Lend-
    Lease program; Pearl
    Harbor; Roosevelt,
    Franklin D.
about, 5–7, **94–97**
and America First
    Committee (AFC),
    11–13
Axis powers in, 14–16
France in, 31–32
Great Britain in, 32–33
Japan in, 38–40
start of, 23
and Thomas Norman, 78

Y

Young, Owen D., 85, 97
Young Plan, 23, 85, **97–98**

Z

Zimmermann, Alfred, 88–89,
    92